RECKLESS

AND OTHER PLAYS

RECKLESS

AND OTHER PLAYS

CRAIG LUCAS

THEATRE COMMUNICATIONS GROUP
NEW YORK

Reckless and Other Plays is published by Theatre Communications Group, Inc.,
520 8th Avenue, 24th Floor, New York, NY 10018–4156

Due to space constraints, credit information for excerpted material
appears at the back of the book.

Cover image: Rothko, Mark (1903–1970) © copyright ARS, NY. "Untitled"
(also known as "Blue, Green, Blue on Blue Ground"). Tempura on paper,
40 1/4″ x 23 3/4″. Collection of The Newark Museum, gift of Mr. Clinton Wilder,
1980. 80.341. Copyright The Newark Museum / Art Resource, NY; The
Newark Museum, Newark, New Jersey, U.S.A.

This publication is made possible in part with public funds from the New York
State Council on the Arts, a State Agency.

TCG books are exclusively distributed to the book trade by Consortium Book
Sales and Distribution, 1045 Westgate Dr., St. Paul, MN 55114.

LIBRARY OF CONGRESS CATALOGING-IN-PUBLICATION DATA

Lucas, Craig.
Reckless, and other plays / by Craig Lucas.
p. cm.
ISBN 1-55936-211-1 (Paperback : alk. paper)
I. Title.
PS3562.U233 R444 2003
812'.54—dc21
2003000820

Cover design by Chip Kidd
Text design and composition by Lisa Govan

First Edition, November 2003

CONTENTS

EACH OF THESE PLAYS was written in the face of calamity. Two are comedies, one a drama, all three tragic.

Reckless came in the midst of sudden deaths of friends and lovers in the early 1980s, a national and personal catastrophe. To this swiftly snowballing nightmare, one was forced to add the monumental indifference of the Reagan administration to a virus soon to infect the globe; each and every one of the million upon million of infections bears witness to the colossus of missed opportunity. *Blue Window* grew in that soil of chattering solipsism, as well as the untapped strengths, even hope, (also) nascent there. *Stranger* was written in the wake of three deaths—triplet baby girls— caused by botched amniocenteses, leaving no recourse for the mother or this father. All three plays have female protagonists facing what might seem insurmountable obstacles:

In *Reckless*, Rachel's dream of a perfect American middle-class existence dies a protracted death, leaving her nearly silent, always listening, strangely serene; she escapes three near-fatal scraps with fate, running and running and getting nowhere as in a nightmare. It is only when she gives up trying, stops running, that she finds the things she thought were lost forever. In facing the inevitability of her suffering, she finds some relief from it.

In *Blue Window*, Libby's struggle to overcome a gruesome tragedy imposed upon her by a careless workman's oversight leaves her at play's end poised perhaps to put the experience behind her: what she has tried to hide from everyone has no hope of disappearing until it has been exposed to the light.

At *Stranger*'s conclusion, Linda is seen irrevocably disfigured by the cruelties visited upon her; she has repeatedly elected for horrific, painful surgery in her endless attempts to wipe out any trace of her earlier pains; the pains she takes to erase her past leave her nowhere to hide but inside the pain itself. She is defined by nothing *but* her suffering. It seems to come as a shock to some that, despite so many cheerful, televised assurances of presidents and talk show hosts, certain experiences are *not* to be overcome. Death, sadly, is not the only irrevocable loss in many lives.

Ghosts of the lost creatures these women might have become, once were, wished to be, are joined by the host of unborn ones waiting to spring into existence out of the choices they do or do not make. These are the real inhabitants of the plays.

From Greek tragedy to our own largely unseen ones, man's ability to choose his or her countenance in the face of fatal blows is the noblest testament to our deepest humanity. Suffering may be inevitable, but what we do about it is not.

Plays exist best in the now. On the page, as literature, they are ghosts of their living selves. *Onstage* they are capable of conveying not only the now of whenever they were written (that long-dead present tense given miraculous re-birth in performance), but also the living presence of possibility.

Human beings, too, are at their best in the now. But when we are told not to live in the past, not to *dwell* there, aren't we so often being enjoined to forget our history?

There is much to be written, to be remembered, and much to be done. And theatre remains one art form which does not yield easily to the trigger-fast repression of corporations and governments; it does not require printing, expensive recording equipment, factories for producing the film, the video, the paper, the computer imaging; it does not rely upon access to the internet, subscribers, advertisers, nor the vast sums of capital to pay the legal fees and buy the satellites to beam it to an intended audience. It can be performed for free in the open air.

As technology penetrates deeper and deeper into the space between us, theatre remains as much *in the now* as any art form could ever be—alive as a kiss.

CRAIG LUCAS
July 4, 2003

RECKLESS

━ The play is dedicated to ━
Daniel Clarke Slautterback

Reckless was first staged, in an earlier form, by The Production Company (Norman René, Artistic Director; Abigail Franklin, Managing Director) in 1983, under the direction of Norman René. Jan Eliasberg directed a South Coast Repertory production in 1985, and Steven Schachter an Atlantic Theater Company staging in 1987.

The first performance of this version was on September 14, 1988, at New York's Circle Repertory Company. Directed by René, the Circle Rep production ran until the end of the year. The sets were designed by Loy Arcenas, costumes by Walker Hicklin, lights by Debra J. Kletter and sound by Chuck London/Stewart Werner. The cast was as follows:

RACHEL	Robin Bartlett
TOM	Michael E. Piontek
LLOYD	John Dossett
POOTY	Welker White
ROY	Kelly Connell
TRISH	Susan Blommaert
DOCTORS ONE THROUGH SIX	Joyce Reehling
TIM TIMKO	Kelly Connell
TALK SHOW HOST	Kelly Connell
DR. HELEN CARROLL	Welker White
WOMAN PATIENT	Susan Blommaert
TOM JR.	Michael E. Piontek

RACHEL	FIRST DERELICT
TOM	SECOND DERELICT
LLOYD	SIXTH DOCTOR
POOTY	TALK SHOW HOST
ROY	SUE
TRISH	MAN IN SKI MASK
FIRST DOCTOR	WOMAN PATIENT
TIM TIMKO	RECEPTIONIST
SECOND DOCTOR	TOM JR.
THIRD DOCTOR	VOICES OF VARIOUS
FOURTH DOCTOR	ANNOUNCERS AND
FIFTH DOCTOR	NEWSCASTERS

Reckless can be performed with as few as seven actors. Tom, Tom Jr. and the Man in Ski Mask are doubled, as are the First through Sixth Doctors.

A solitude ten thousand fathoms deep
Sustains the bed on which we lie, my dear;
Although I love you, you will have to leap;
Our dream of safety has to disappear.

—W.H. AUDEN

The glow of the television. Rachel at the window in her night-gown; Tom in bed.

RACHEL: I think I'm more excited than they are. I really do. I think we just have kids so that we can tell them all about Santa Claus and have an excuse to believe it all ourselves again. I really do. They are so excited. I remember that feeling so clearly. I didn't think I could ever sleep. And I remember pinching myself and pinching myself to stay awake so I could hear the reindeers' footsteps, you know? I wanted to believe it so badly. I think that was the last year I did . . . Oh God . . . Is it still snowing? Why don't you turn the sound up? *(Tom shakes his head, stares at the screen)* Oh, it's coming down like crazy. You can hear it, can't you, when it gets deep like this? It just swallows up all the sound and you feel like you've been wrapped up in the hands of a big, sweet, giant, white . . . monster. Good monster. He's going to carry us away into a dream. My family always had champagne first thing before we opened our presents—I mean, in the morning, you know. I always loved that. I felt like such an adult having champagne and I remember saying to my mother that the bubbles in the champagne looked like snow if you turned your head upside down. I remember thinking I wanted to live in Alaska because it always snowed and Santa was up there, so it must always be Christmas . . . You're my Santa Claus. And our two elves. I'm having one of my euphoria attacks. I think I'm going to be terminally happy, you'd better watch out, it's catching. Highly contagious . . . What's the matter? Just sleepy? *(He nods)* Can we listen for a second, I won't stay up all night, I promise.

(Rachel switches on the TV.)

ANNOUNCER'S VOICE: —as they raise their small voices in joyous celebration once more.

(The Vienna Boys Choir is heard singing.)

RACHEL: Oh God, look at those faces. I feel so sorry for Jeanette and Freddie sometimes. These things happen for a reason, I know, but . . . I always think if something happened to us I'd want them to raise the boys.

ANNOUNCER'S VOICE: This is David Harbinger from Vienna.

SECOND ANNOUNCER'S VOICE: And in a bizarre note this Christmas Eve: an Albanian woman fled across the border into Yugoslavia where it is said she gave birth to a two-headed child today. Both mother and son are reported to be in stable condition. According to spokesmen, the woman is either unwilling or unable to speak. So far there has been no explanation for her flight. Well, whoever's dreaming of a white Christmas doesn't have to dream tonight. Weatherman Sheldon Strafford has the story.

RACHEL *(Overlapping)*: Isn't that awful?

(Tom begins to cry.)

THIRD ANNOUNCER'S VOICE: Bill, we thought this low-pressure front might never move out, but as you can see it finally has and tiny tots and snowmen should be playing together in the streets by dawn.

RACHEL *(Continuing over TV)*: What's the matter? . . . Oh, honey, it's just the news, come on, it's not real. We'll turn it off, see? It's gone. *(She switches off TV)* Don't be upset on Christmas. Everything's great, I'm here and everything's fine.

TOM: I took a contract out on your life.

RACHEL: What do you mean? Life insurance?

TOM: A contract on your life.

RACHEL: This is the sickest joke, I'm sorry. I don't care what's bothering you, you could just come out with it—

TOM: All right, listen to me—

RACHEL: You get these idiotic ideas of what's funny—

TOM: I want you to listen to me if you've never listened to me in your life—

RACHEL: It's Christmas Eve!

TOM: In five minutes a man's going to break through the bay windows downstairs, I'm sorry this is happening this way, it's a stupid solution and we should have talked it out, but it's done and he'll be here in less than five minutes. I want you to put on your coat and some slippers, you can climb out this window over the garage and run over to Jeanette's. When he's gone I'll call you and we can talk about it.

RACHEL *(Overlapping)*: Tom Fitsimmons, I know you and I think this is really off the mark, I'm sorry. Fun is fun . . . I'm going to sleep in the other bedroom.

TOM: Rachel! Listen to me now if you want to live!

RACHEL: You're hurting me.

TOM: I paid this man, he's a professional, I cannot take it back. All right, look: *(He produces a handgun)* This is a .38. It has no bullets. It's staged to look like he broke in and I pulled a gun and he killed you—a thief—an accident. I'm sorry, you can't be here, we'll talk it all out in a little while when he's gone.

RACHEL: You're frightening me.

TOM: I'll tell him you went to stay with your mother. He has his money, he can go. Tell Jeanette we had a fight, it doesn't matter, I'll call you when he's gone.

RACHEL: This is so mean.

(The sound of glass shattering below. Rachel climbs out the window.)

TOM: Go! He won't see you! Stay in the dark! Keep in the shadows!

SCENE 2

Rachel at a pay phone in her robe and slippers. Snow.

RACHEL: Jeanette? Rachel. Merry Christmas . . . No, everything's great, but listen, would you and Freddie mind taking a little spin down here to the Arco station at Route 3 and Carl Bluestein Boulevard? No, no, nothing like that, I just came outside . . . Oh, isn't it? It's beautiful, uh-huh, listen, Jeanette, Tom took a . . . Tom . . . It's so ridiculous. He took a contract out on my life . . . A contract? . . . Uh-huh. Right. And, I mean the man broke in downstairs so I thought I'd better go out of the house, so I climbed out over the garage and I was afraid to ring your bell, because you have all those pretty lights and I was afraid he might be following my tracks in the snow—

(Lloyd approaches in the darkness.)

—and so I though maybe you'd just zip down here and we'd all have some eggnog or something, what do you

say? . . . Jeane—? No . . . No, I know, I am, I'm a kid-
der . . . But—Merry Christmas to you too, Jeanette,
please don't . . .

(Jeanette has hung up. Rachel turns, sees Lloyd, screams.)

AAAAAAGH! NO, MY GOD! PLEASE!

LLOYD *(Overlapping her, backing up)*: Hey. Hey.

RACHEL: Oh, I'm sorry. Did you want to use the phone?
Please, go right ahead.

LLOYD: I'm just trying to find a gas station.

RACHEL: This is the gas station, right here, you found one.
For *gas*! Oh, not on Christmas Eve, maybe up on the
turnpike . . . Merry Christmas.

LLOYD: Merry Christmas. You need a lift?

RACHEL: No. Yes. No.

LLOYD: It's no problem.

RACHEL: No. Thank you.

LLOYD: You're sure?

RACHEL: No, thank you. I mean, yes—I . . .

LLOYD: Come on, hop in.

SCENE 3

In the car.

RACHEL: Thank you.

LLOYD: Better?

RACHEL: Yes.

LLOYD: Where you headed? . . . Some night.

RACHEL: Yes. Yes. Christmas. I love Christmas.

LLOYD: Yeah.

RACHEL: Snow . . . You have a family?

LLOYD: No . . . Well, you know . . . You?

RACHEL: No . . . No, no. *(Her wedding ring)* Oh this? This is
just costume. I just wear this, see? *(Tosses the ring out
the window)* Good-bye! That felt wonderful. Maybe

you should just let me off up at the, uh . . . Well, I can get off anywhere. Oh, you wanted to get gas. Where do you live?

LLOYD: Springfield.

RACHEL: Springfield . . . The field of spring.

LLOYD: You and your husband have a fight or something?

RACHEL: I'm not married. You married? . . . You have a girl-friend.

LLOYD: Just Pooty.

RACHEL: Pooty . . . Pooty . . . My son does the cutest thing. I was married before. He's four and a half. My son has custody—my father—oh God. My son is four and a half, my husband has custody, my father is dead. And he does this thing—there are two boys, but Jeremy's just three. But Tom—Tom Junior, not my husband, Tom Senior—Tom Junior is always firing everybody, you know, if he doesn't like what you're doing. He'll say to his babysitter who is usually my friend Jeanette who can't have kids of her own because of this thing in her—uterus—he'll say to Jeanette, you know, um, "You're fired, Jeanette!" You know? Just because she wants to put him to bed or something. And just today he fired me. I mean, on Christmas Eve. I said, "You're gonna fire your own mother?" "That's right," he said, "you're fired!" So.

LLOYD: Now you're fired.

RACHEL: Now I'm fired. What does Pooty do? Is that her name?

LLOYD: Pooty.

RACHEL: What does she do?

LLOYD: She works.

RACHEL: Oh, that's good. Do you work? *(He nods)* Same place Pooty works? *(He nods)* Now how did I know that? Not me, I've never worked. *(Pause)* Did you tell me your name?

LLOYD: Lloyd.

RACHEL: Lloyd.

LLOYD: Bophtelophti.

RACHEL: Bophtelophti. Isn't *that* an interesting name. I'm—
Mary Ellen Sissle. Is my maiden name.

LLOYD: Nice to meet you.

RACHEL: Don't let go of the wheel! Nice to meet you, too.
My father always said, "Don't interfere with the driver
whilst the vehicle is in motion." You think I'm escaped
from an institution, don't you?

LLOYD: Are you? *(She laughs)* What's so funny?

RACHEL: Nothing, I'm sorry, I just suddenly saw . . . I mean,
me in my housedress and my slippers out in the snow.

LLOYD: Oh, it's cool.

RACHEL: Yes, it was. I've always wanted to do something like
that, you know? Run away in the middle of the night in
your slip and your slippers with some strange man
who would ruin your reputation and disappoint your
parents terribly and disappoint your friends and just
make you really happy. Well, I think we get these ideas
from rock-and-roll songs, actually.

LLOYD: Right.

RACHEL: Which is why I would never really do anything like
that except here I am. But, no, I mean, this isn't really
like that, I just meant running away and becoming . . .
Well, I don't know what I thought I'd become. But
running away. And here I am.

LLOYD: Here you are.

RACHEL: On my way to . . .

LLOYD: Meet Pooty.

RACHEL: Meet Pooty . . . *(Pause)* Lloyd?

LLOYD: Yeah?

RACHEL: Do you think we ever really know people? I mean,
I know we know people . . .

LLOYD: You mean really.

RACHEL: But really.

LLOYD: You mean *know* them.

RACHEL: Do you think?

LLOYD: Well . . . I don't know.

RACHEL: I don't know either. I mean, I suppose I know lots
of people.

LLOYD: Sure you do.

RACHEL: And you know lots of people.

LLOYD: Pooty.

RACHEL: We live our lives and we know lots of people and . . . I don't know what I'm saying. D'you get a Christmas tree? *(He nods)* That's nice. "Oh, Christmas tree! Oh Christmas tree . . ." *(She stops singing, near tears)*

LLOYD: It's all right.

RACHEL: I know . . .

LLOYD: The holidays can be tough sometimes . . . You see your parents?

RACHEL: Not since they died . . .

LLOYD: You'll spend Christmas with us.

SCENE 4

Living room.

RACHEL: Don't wake her.

LLOYD: Oh, she'll be glad to meet you. *(He goes off)*

RACHEL: I love your house . . . Be calm . . .

LLOYD *(Back)*: She'll be out in a sec.

RACHEL: This is so Christmassy.

LLOYD: How 'bout a rum toddy? . . . Comin' right up! *(He goes off again)*

RACHEL: This is so lovely . . .

LLOYD *(From off)*: Glad to have the company.

(Pooty enters in her wheelchair.)

RACHEL: Surprise! Hello, Rachel—Mary Ellen! Rachel May Ellen, the Rachel is silent. Nice to meet you. This is so nice. I hope I'm not, you know. I feel . . . Well, actually, my house burned down and Lloyd was kind enough to say I could stop in. You know, stop up. So, I'm, uh, not . . .

(No reaction. Lloyd returns.)

LLOYD: You have to keep your face towards her so she can read your lips.

RACHEL: Oh, she's deaf. You're deaf! I'm sorry, not that you're deaf, but . . . I just *love* your house.

(Lloyd signs for Pooty.)

LLOYD: The one and only Pooty-Poot-Pooter.

RACHEL: Yesssss.

LLOYD *(Spelling the name)*: Mary Ellen Sizzler.

RACHEL: Well. Did you slip on the ice, it looks like.

LLOYD: She's paraplegic.

RACHEL: Paraplegic! Oh, paraplegic.

LLOYD: Paraplegic.

RACHEL: I have to keep my face this way, don't I? . . . Um . . . Tell me, Pooty—

LLOYD: I'm just gonna check on the toddies. *(He goes out again)*

RACHEL: —what kind of name is that? Your name. It's so unusual. *Your name!*

(Pooty jots on a piece of paper.)

(Reads) "Pooty." Uh-huh. You know, I was just saying before . . .

(Lloyd returns with two glasses.)

LLOYD: She talk your ear off?

RACHEL: Thank you.

LLOYD: Pooter Bear.

RACHEL: Aren't you having any?

LLOYD: Never touch the stuff. Cheers.

RACHEL: Cheers. Sure there isn't any poison in here?

(Rachel smiles, drinks. Lloyd and Pooty confer in sign.)

Mmmmm . . . Isn't that beautiful the way you do that?

LLOYD: All right, everybody, have a seat. Time to open presents.

RACHEL: I'll watch. This'll be fun.

LLOYD *(Handing her a gift)*: Merry Christmas. From us. Open it.

RACHEL: But I didn't get anybody anything.

LLOYD: Go on.

RACHEL: Oh, I think this was meant for someone else. This is so strange. *(Opens the package; it's a shower massage)* Look! Aren't you both so nice? Thank you.

LLOYD: You like it?

RACHEL: Ohhh, *like* it?

LLOYD: Okay, who's next?

RACHEL: Wait, okay, I know what I want to do. Now I'm sorry I didn't get a chance to wrap this, but . . . *(Gives Pooty her necklace)* Merry Christmas! Isn't this fun? I'll put it on.

LLOYD: She says you didn't have to do that.

RACHEL: Of course I didn't have to do that. You didn't have to ask a woman in her slippers to come spend Christmas with you either. I could be a mass killer. I could be anybody . . . I could be anybody.

SCENE 5

RACHEL *(On the telephone)*: Jeanette? Yes, Happy New Year, how are you? I'm great. So how was your Christmas, what did you get? . . . What? Oh, right now? Oh, I'm just up at my cousin's, you know. Of course I have a cousin, what do you mean you didn't know I had a cousin? Everybody has cousins. Where? I don't know, Jeanette, right up Route—what difference does it make? But— . . . No, I'm fine. Jeanette. Do I sound fine? Do I sound fine? Well. Oh shoot, here comes my bus, but listen do me a favor? No, I will, but—I can't, Jeanette, but would you look in on the boys for me? When you get a chance? You will? Thanks, but listen, they're closing the doors, I've got to go. Okay. Bye, Jeanette! *(She hangs up)*

SCENE 6

Living room.

LLOYD: Earth to Mary Ellen?

RACHEL: Hm?

LLOYD: Hungry?

RACHEL: No, thanks. Oh, I'll cook, how's that? What would you like?

LLOYD: What do you make?

RACHEL: Whatever you want, just name it. It's yours.

LLOYD: Whatever we want?

RACHEL: Whatever you want.

LLOYD *(After conferring in sign with Pooty)*: Well, we've discussed it.

RACHEL: Uh-huh?

LLOYD: And we both want you to stay here.

RACHEL: For dinner?

LLOYD: For as long as you like.

RACHEL: Oh no, I couldn't.

LLOYD: Why?

RACHEL: Well, I mean, I could, but I can't.

LLOYD: Well?

RACHEL: No. Thank you, though. Very much.

LLOYD: Why can't you?

RACHEL: Because.

LLOYD: Because why?

RACHEL: Because.

LLOYD: Because why?

RACHEL: Lloyd.

LLOYD: I'm serious.

RACHEL: Because I have to get a job, I have to get some shoes, I can't just move in.

(Pooty exits.)

LLOYD: Why not?
RACHEL: Pooty, come on!
LLOYD: She can't hear you, she's deaf.
RACHEL: Thank you, Lloyd, I'm having enough trouble as it is.
LLOYD: Well?
RACHEL: Because.
LLOYD: Because why?
RACHEL: This is the way children talk.
LLOYD: So?
RACHEL: So? So's your old man. Just because.

(Pooty returns with her lap filled with shoes.)

And what is this? Shoes. Oh God, I love you both so much, I do. Why are you doing this?
LLOYD: Because.
RACHEL: And where *are* we, anyway? Where is Springfield?
LLOYD: We've got an atlas.
RACHEL: I mean, do you people even have identification? My mother may not even let me play with you. She's very fussy, you know.

(Lloyd opens the atlas.)

LLOYD: Here . . . Hold on . . .
RACHEL: I believe you.
LLOYD: Springfield. If you lived here you'd be home by now.
RACHEL *(Holding the book)*: Look how big the world is: it's all in this book . . . Oh Lloyd . . . I would love to stay here, you know that. I would love to start my whole life right here at this second.
LLOYD: Why can't you?
RACHEL: Because. I'd have to get a job.

SCENE 7

The office. Trish at a computer terminal. Roy and Rachel standing.

ROY: Hands Across the Sea is a not-for-profit, humanitarian foundation.

RACHEL *(To Trish)*: Hi.

ROY: This does not mean we get away with murder.

RACHEL: Uh-huh.

ROY: Any of us. We all work very long, very hard hours for very little pay. Trish Hammers, this is our new clerk, Mary Ellen Sissle.

RACHEL: How do you do?

ROY: Americans lead soft, sheltered lives, I'm sure I don't need to tell you.

RACHEL: No.

ROY: We are barely cognizant of the human misery as it exists on this planet today, under our very noses too.

RACHEL: Really.

ROY: If I could pay you less than minimum wage, I would, believe me. Medical research, building a school in a foreign desert with illiterate, unskilled, underfed igno-ramuses . . . Well, it's expensive. Clinics, halfway houses, physical therapy labs where Lloyd and Pooty work—

RACHEL: Right.

ROY: Adult education programs, drug rehabilitation . . . These are your insurance forms. Fill these out and give them to Mr. Seakins. Then ask Trish for some documents to process, she'll explain how you do that. Any other questions come straight to me.

RACHEL: Great.

ROY: So, enjoy.

RACHEL: I will, thanks.

ROY: Welcome aboard.

RACHEL: Thank you.

(Roy goes out.)

He seems nice. *(She sits; her chair collapses)* Whoops! I'm going to need insurance. Do you know how I, uh . . . ? *(No response)* Never mind, I got it. *(Adjusts seat)* So how was your Christmas? You see your family?

TRISH: I'm not a big fan of Christmas.

RACHEL: Oh. Parents put coals in your stocking one year or something?

TRISH: My parents were killed when I was six months old.

RACHEL: Oh, I'm terribly sorry.

TRISH: Why? You didn't do it

RACHEL: No, I know. *(Realizing her chair has sunk down again)* Oh, God, I thought I was getting shorter. Is there another chair, do you know? . . . This is fine. *(Starts to fill in forms)* Who's Mistress Eakins? I'm sorry, I'm supposed to take this to Mistress Eakins, do you know where she is? . . . Mistress Eakins? Do you know what I'm talking about?

TRISH: No.

RACHEL: Mistress Eakins, I think he said.

TRISH: Mr. Seakins.

RACHEL: Oh. I thought he said Mistress Eakins. I thought that was kind of a strange name, but mine is not to reason why, mine is just . . . So where is he? Mr. Seakins.

TRISH: I'll give it to him.

RACHEL: No, I don't mind.

(Trish takes the forms from her.)

Well. So do you have any kids or anything?

TRISH: No.

RACHEL: No family?

TRISH: Nope.

RACHEL: Brothers and sisters? *(Trish shakes her head)* Wow, you get your own screen and everything, huh?

TRISH: All right. I'd like you to take the white sheets, transfer everything onto the green sheets and staple them together. File everything in alpha-numerical order in the cabinets marked "Hardcopy." After that we'll go

through the storeroom and if there's time I'll show you
where the microfilm records are kept.

RACHEL: Great.

SCENE 8

Living room.

LLOYD: So how was it?

RACHEL *(Signing to Pooty throughout)*: It was great.

LLOYD: You liked Trish?

RACHEL: Oh, yeah. Now she's in charge of what again?

LLOYD: All the budget.

RACHEL: Oh.

LLOYD: And she's pretty convinced she doesn't need an
assistant, either.

RACHEL: Oh, really? Well.

LLOYD: She'll loosen up.

RACHEL *(To Pooty)*: So then she does the payroll? . . . How do
you say payroll, Lloyd?

LLOYD: I don't know. Ask her.

RACHEL: No, come on.

LLOYD: Spell it. I'll be out in the woodshed if anybody needs
me.

RACHEL: You're just trying to turn me into a deaf girl, I know.

LLOYD *(As he exits)*: I can't hear you!

(Rachel and Pooty sign for a moment.)

RACHEL: She does. She seems kind of tight-lipped.

POOTY: She is. Now, listen, he can't know. *(Rachel is dumb-
founded)* It would break his heart . . . I'm sorry I didn't
say anything before.

RACHEL: Oh, listen . . . you know.

POOTY: When I lost the use of my legs a friend drove me up
here to Springfield to take a look at this place where
they worked with the handicapped. I watched the

physical therapists working with the patients and there was one: I remember he was working with a quadriplegic. I thought he was the most beautiful man I'd ever seen. A light shining out through his skin. And I thought if I couldn't be with him I'd die. But I knew I would just be one more crippled dame as far as he was concerned, so my friend helped to get me registered as deaf and disabled. I used to teach sign language to the hearing impaired. I thought if I were somehow needier than the rest I would get special attention. I realized soon enough: everyone gets special attention where Lloyd is concerned. But by then it was too late. He was in love with me, with my honesty. He learned to sign; he told me how he'd run away from a bad marriage and changed his name so he wouldn't have to pay child support. He got me a job at Hands Across the Sea and I couldn't bring myself to tell him that I had another name and another life, that I'd run away too, because I owed the government so much money and wasn't able to pay after the accident. I believe in honesty. I believe in total honesty. And I need him and he needs me to be the person he thinks I am and I am that person, I really am that person. I'm a crippled deaf girl, short and stout. Here is my wheelchair, here is my mouth.

RACHEL: I'm not judging you.

POOTY: When he goes out I babble. I recite poetry I remember from grade school. I talk back to the television. I even call people on the phone and say it's a wrong number just to have a conversation. I'm afraid I'm going to open my mouth to scream one day and . . . *(She does; no sound)*

(Lloyd returns with fresh-chopped kindling.)

LLOYD: Keep it down in here. How's it going?

RACHEL: Great. It's pretty good.

LLOYD: I'm sorry, I didn't hear you.
RACHEL: It's pretty good, I say.
LLOYD: I still can't hear you.
RACHEL: I said it's—
LLOYD: *WHAT?*
RACHEL: Oh.

(Rachel signs. Lloyd signs and goes out again.)

POOTY: He was the first person who ever heard me. Really heard me. And I never had to make a sound. You mustn't ever tell him.
RACHEL: I won't. I think people who love each other, whatever way they love each other, nobody should say it's right or wrong. *(Pause)* Do you think Lloyd . . . ? I mean, do you think he would ever . . . hurt you? I mean, not hurt you, but . . .
POOTY: Want to?
RACHEL: Want to, say.
POOTY: Sure. It wouldn't be love, would it?
RACHEL: Would it?
POOTY: Why?
RACHEL: Oh, I don't know.
POOTY: Did someone try to hurt you?
RACHEL: Oh, no, no, no, no.
POOTY: Who tried to hurt you?
RACHEL: Nobody.
POOTY: You can tell me.
RACHEL: Tom wouldn't do anything like that. He wouldn't.
POOTY: Who's Tom?
RACHEL *(Overlapping)*: Forget I mentioned it. Really.

(Beat.)

POOTY: I think you should talk to someone about this, don't you?

SCENE 9

Doctor's office.

DOCTOR: Go on.

RACHEL: Well, I don't know. There's really no problem.

DOCTOR: No?

RACHEL: No. I don't know . . .

DOCTOR: What are you thinking?

RACHEL: I don't know. About Christmas, I guess.

DOCTOR: Do you feel like telling me about it?

RACHEL: Well, last Christmas? Christmas Eve? My husband
Tom is all tucked into bed like a little kid and our two
boys are in their beds, I've just tucked them in, and
I tell Tom how perfect it all seems, I've never been so
happy, which is true. And . . . Well, my father was aller-
gic to dogs, you know, and Tom didn't like puppies, so
I never said anything about wanting a puppy, but I was
thinking about it. And I was looking out into the snow
and talking about Alaska or something, but I was
thinking about how people in books and movies are
always getting puppies on Christmas and you never
see anybody having to clean up the . . .

DOCTOR: Shit.

RACHEL: Or get hit by cars. You always see them with a big
red bow and the kids are smiling and—but I didn't say
anything, I was just thinking it. I didn't want Tom to
feel guilty if he hadn't gotten me a puppy which I knew
he hadn't because he hates them, so it was just a private
little something I was thinking about and that's all
I needed really was to think about it and rub its little
imaginary ears. And we were watching the news,
I remember, and suddenly I realize Tom's upset. So
naturally I assume he knows I really want a puppy, so
I go to comfort him, because I don't care about it,
really, if it's going to make him unhappy, I don't even
mention it, I just give him a big hug and tell him it's

24

Christmas and be happy and he says he's taken a contract out on my life.

DOCTOR: This upset you.

RACHEL: Maybe I'm overreacting. Or he's kidding, which
I think he must be. But anyway, I wind up spending
Christmas with this man I meet at the Arco station
and his girlfriend who is crippled and deaf, she says,
you know, with hand signals until suddenly she just
turns to me and starts saying how she had to pretend
she was deaf to get the attention of this man we're all
living with who's changed his name and run away and
she's changed her name and I've changed my name
and we're all working in the same place and she's
telling me all these secrets and all of a sudden she says,
"Why don't you talk to a psychiatrist?"

DOCTOR: And here you are.

RACHEL: Here I am.

DOCTOR: When did you have this dream?

SCENE 10

The office.

TRISH: I'm going to have to take an early lunch today, Mary
Ellen.

RACHEL: Okay.

TRISH: So if you'll hold down the fort.

RACHEL: Anything I can do for you on the computer or anything?

TRISH: No, thanks.

RACHEL: Well, anytime you want to teach me.

TRISH: I think you probably have enough work to keep you
busy.

*(Trish goes out. Rachel looks around, then moves over to
Trish's seat. Lloyd enters.)*

LLOYD: Hi.

RACHEL: Hi.

LLOYD: Mind if I join you?

RACHEL: No. Have a seat.

LLOYD: Learning Lotus?

RACHEL: No, what's that?

LLOYD: Oh, that's the software.

RACHEL: What's software?

LLOYD: Oh, that's what tells the computer what to do.

RACHEL: Oh.

LLOYD: I don't even know if that's what we use.

RACHEL: You know? In all the months I've been here Trish has never shown me how to do anything except file and take care of the storeroom and stuff like that.

LLOYD: Well, give her time.

RACHEL: Yeah. I guess. She has no family.

LLOYD: Yeah.

RACHEL: She says.

LLOYD: What do you mean?

RACHEL: I don't know. Just for all we know she could have ten families and a trail of broken hearts behind her, right? Who knows?

LLOYD: What else have you and Pooty been discussing?

RACHEL: Nothing.

LLOYD: Anything you'd like to ask me personally?

RACHEL: Oh, I wasn't even thinking about that.

LLOYD: Yes, I left my family. No, they don't know where I am—

RACHEL: No, I wasn't asking any of this.

LLOYD *(Overlapping)*: No, I don't pay child support, no, Bophtelophti is not my real name—

RACHEL: Please, Lloyd.

LLOYD: My real name is Boyd T. Theophillo . . .

RACHEL: The past is irrelevant. It's something you wake up from.

LLOYD: I walked out on a woman with multiple sclerosis and two children, one of them brain damaged, because I was too drunk to see him playing in the snow and I ran over him with the snow blower. I left them with no money and no way to feed themselves, moved as far away as I possibly could, changed my name, took the cash I'd stolen from the savings account to pay for the kids' education and put myself through school, so that I could become a physical therapist and work with multiple sclerosis victims and the occasional brain-damaged child with resultant motor-skill difficulties, none of whom held the slightest interest for me other than to remind me of what I could never escape as long as I live. And let's see. I married a nice crippled, deaf girl and I don't drink anymore. The past is some-thing you wake up to. It's the nightmare you wake up to every day.

RACHEL: Well, these things happen for a reason, I believe that, I'm sorry, I do. And you're not helping anybody by punishing yourself. Why don't you pay back the money and say you're sorry?

LLOYD: It was thirty-five thousand dollars.

RACHEL: So? Big deal. People win that on game shows.

SCENE 11

TV studio.

ANNOUNCER: And here's your host, Tim Timko!

TIM: Okay, here we go, how does this game work, where are we? Oh, yes, it all comes back to me, like last night, who was that girl? Okay, enough of that, it's good to be back, let's see who's here.

(House lights.)

Remember, all you need's a mother, a wife, and the crazy idea that you could tell the difference. Looks like an awful lot of bag ladies slipped in here. How're we all doin'?

(Crowd response.)

Anybody want to play this thing? What's it called? Your Brother's Wife? Your Sister's Best Friend's Mother-in-Law?

(Sign lights up. Rachel, Lloyd and Pooty are in the audience, dressed as the solar system with cardboard and papier-mâché constructions over their heads.)

Your Mother or Your Wife?! Ah! Wait. *(He makes his way over to the oddly costumed trio)* Wait, wait a minute, I know what I like and don't tell me now, you folks are dressed as the solar system, aren't you?

LLOYD: That's right, Tim.

TIM: This looks like the planet Earth down here.

LLOYD: That's my mother, Tim.

TIM: Mother Earth.

LLOYD: Right.

TIM: I'll bet your world revolves around your sun, too, doesn't it. What's your name, sir?

LLOYD: Lloyd.

TIM: You have a last name, Lloyd?

LLOYD: Bophtelophti.

TIM: Where you from, Lloyd?

LLOYD: Springfield?

TIM: Springfield? Massachusetts? *(To Rachel)* And you must be the little lady.

LLOYD: That's right, Tim.

RACHEL: Venus.

TIM: Ah. "One touch of."

LLOYD: That's right.

TIM: Well, you've met our requirements, Lloyd.

LLOYD: I should tell you, Tim, my mother is deaf. But my wife speaks sign language.

TIM: So she can translate. Okay. Come on up and get set to play *Your Mother or Your Wife!*

(Music, applause. Lloyd, Rachel, and Pooty are led onstage.)

All right, correctly identify which of these lovely ladies answered each of three scintillating questions supplied by our studio audience made up entirely of Nobel Prize Laureates by the way— *(To someone in the audience)* What, you don't believe me? Get him out of here. And you can win yourself up to twenty thousand dollars, Lloyd, and a chance to play for our grand prize.

ANNOUNCER: Tim, the Bophtelophtis will be playing for a grand cash total of one hundred thousand dollars.

TIM: A hundred grand. Are you ready for our glass booth?

LLOYD: I guess so, Tim.

TIM: Then take him away.

(Lloyd is led offstage.)

Never to be heard from again. *(To Rachel and Pooty)* Good evening, ladies.

RACHEL: It's great to be here, Tim!

TIM: You're going to translate.

RACHEL: That's right.

TIM: No funny business. Anybody here speaks deaf, keep an eye on these two. All right, Venus, first question.

RACHEL: Okay.

TIM: Would you say that Lloyd is more like a Ping-Pong ball or a paper clip? Mmmmm.

RACHEL: I'll say a Ping-Pong ball.

TIM: Any particular reason?

RACHEL: He bounces around a lot?

TIM: He does? Okay. Mom? Is Lloyd more like a Ping-Pong ball or a paper clip, would you say? Two Ps . . .

(Rachel and Pooty confer in sign.)

RACHEL: She says a paper clip.

TIM: Because?

RACHEL: Because he holds the family together.

TIM: Awww, that's—disgusting. No, I'm just teasing you. Question number two: Mom first this time. If Lloyd were a salad dressing, what flavor would he be? If blank were a salad dressing . . .

RACHEL: She says blue cheese.

TIM: He's getting a little moldy? But okay, Venus?

RACHEL: I'll say blue cheese.

TIM: Blue cheese it is. Ladies, third question: If you could choose between your husband leaving you for another woman or, in Mom's case her son leaving her for another mom? . . . *(Looks to the control booth)* Guys, this question doesn't make sense. What's he gonna do, get another mother? . . . Judges say fly with it. All right—between your husband leaving you for another woman or staying together, knowing he doesn't love you, Venus, which would it be? . . .

RACHEL: I'd have to say another woman.

TIM: Another woman. Mom? Between losing your son to another mother or knowing he didn't love you. All right, fair enough.

RACHEL: She says another mother.

TIM: "M" is for the many ways. Ladies, for our grand prize: Who does Lloyd love most, you or Mom?

RACHEL: His mother.

TIM: And Mom? This should be interesting.

(Rachel and Pooty confer. Pooty points to Rachel.)

And she says you! Okay, we'll be right back with the three happy Boopy-Boppies after this word from the good folks at Nu-Soft. Don't go away.

(Lights change; Lloyd is escorted onstage.)

ANNOUNCER: We're going right on. Ten seconds.

TIM *(To Rachel)*: Say your name for me.

RACHEL: Bophtelophti.

TIM: Bophtelophti.

(Lights restore.)

ANNOUNCER: Five, four, three . . . Rolling.

TIM: And we're back with the Bophtelophtis from Spring-field, Massachusetts. Bophtelophti, is that Polish?

RACHEL: Yes, T—

LLOYD *(Simultaneously)*: No, well, it's—

RACHEL: It's . . .

LLOYD: Welsh, actually.

RACHEL: Welsh and Polish.

TIM: Welsh and Polish. How long've you been married?

LLOYD: Ten . . .

RACHEL: Years.

TIM: Ten years. Any kids so far?

LLOYD: No.

RACHEL: But . . .

LLOYD: We're hoping, Tim.

TIM: Well, good luck to you. Because you're gonna need it! Okay, here we go, round two, Lloyd, for five thousand dollars: When asked if you reminded them of a paper clip or a Ping-Pong ball, who said "paper clip" and I quote, "Because he holds the family together." Your mother or your wife.

LLOYD: Boy . . . My mother?

(Rachel hops up and down and claps.)

TIM: Right you are if you think you are, Lloyd.

LLOYD: Okay.

TIM: For ten thousand dollars, when asked what type of salad dressing you reminded them of, who said "blue cheese"? Your mother or your wife.

LLOYD: That's my favorite.

TIM: Nobody's interested in your personal life, Lloyd. No, take your time.

LLOYD: I'll say both.

TIM: Both it is for a quick ten grand! All right, for twenty thousand dollars and a chance to lose it all, Lloyd: Which . . . wait, let me get this straight. Which of the women in your life said they would rather lose you to another woman, wife or mother as the case may be, than believe you to be unhappy in their home. Mother Earth or the Venus de Milo, Lloyd. Lose you to another woman . . .

LLOYD: Both?

TIM: Both it is! Congratulations, Lloyd Bophtelophti from Warsaw, Wales, you've just won twenty thousand dollars and a chance to go home before you ruin your marriage.

LLOYD: No, we want to keep going.

TIM: Remember, if you miss this one, we keep it all, Lloyd, but you do go away with a free home version of your mother and your wife.

LLOYD: We'll play.

TIM: He says he'll play. All right, no eye contact now, no help from the studio audience please, Lloyd, for one hundred thousand dollars *in cash*, we asked your mother and your wife: Who does Lloyd love the most? Who said—keep breathing, Lloyd—you love your wife the most? Your mother, your wife or your mother *and* your wife, it could be both. Don't think too hard, Lloyd . . . Your mother, your wife or your mother and your wife . . . I'm sorry, we're running out of time, we'll have to have an answer, Lloyd.

LLOYD: My mother.

TIM: Your mother!

(Lights flash. Audience screams. Rachel, Lloyd and Pooty express their enthusiasm.)

For one hundred thousand dollars, Lloyd Bophtelophti from Springfield, you've said the magic word, take the money, be happy, this is Tim Timko saying good night, we'll see you next week with your mother, your wife, your mistress, whoever else you got out there . . .

ANNOUNCER *(Under)*: For tickets to *Your Mother or Your Wife* write your name and address on a postcard and mail it to, *Your Mother or Your Wife*, Box 1224, New Hope Station, New York, New York . . . *(His voice fades)*

SCENE 12

The office.

TRISH: How much?

RACHEL: A hundred thousand dollars.

TRISH: You're kidding.

RACHEL: I'm not.

TRISH: That's . . .

RACHEL: Incredible, isn't it?

TRISH: It's incredible.

RACHEL: It's incredible. And you know what the moral is?

TRISH: What's the moral?

RACHEL: You can't be afraid.

TRISH: No.

RACHEL: These things happen for a reason, I keep saying it. I mean, we're all so afraid to take chances and what have we got to lose? We're all going to be dead in a hundred years anyway.

TRISH: This is true.

(Pause.)

RACHEL: Trish?

TRISH: Uh-huh?

RACHEL: Remember when I first came here? . . . Wow, it's almost a year ago now, isn't it?

TRISH: That's right.

RACHEL: You didn't like me, did you?

TRISH: Oh.

RACHEL: No, come on, it's all right.

TRISH: Well, I don't always warm up to people right away.

RACHEL: Oh, I know. But I think it's also because you thought I just wasn't smart enough to handle anything very complicated, didn't you?

TRISH: No.

RACHEL: Well, I decided to take the bull by the horns anyway, and I've sort of been teaching myself about the computer.

TRISH: You have?

RACHEL: When you go to lunch. Look. I got this book on Lotus and I learned how to call up the menu and the file directory and everything.

TRISH: Great.

RACHEL: And I even figured out about the separate accounts you have filed that don't appear on the main index. You know, like the one that's attached to the Christmas fund as a footnote.

TRISH: How'd you figure that out?

RACHEL: Well, I was just, you know—I was trying to figure out what the password was and I was playing around with anagrams and stuff and your name spells "shirt," I'm sure you know, because you used it for the footnote file.

TRISH: Good for you.

RACHEL: Yeah. My dad and I used to like to play word games and things when I was little . . . Anyway . . . You're not mad, are you?

TRISH: No, why should I be mad?

RACHEL: Oh, I don't know. Actually, some of the math doesn't add up either, but . . .

SCENE 13

Doctor's office.

DOCTOR: In the dream . . .

RACHEL: Uh-huh.

DOCTOR: You pretend to be the wife and Pooty . . . Pooty?

RACHEL: Right.

DOCTOR: Pooty is an unusual name.

RACHEL: Mm-*hm*.

DOCTOR: Pooty pretends to be the mother. *(Pause)* Do you think there's any significance to that?

RACHEL: No. I mean, you can't go on the show unless you have a mother and a wife. That's just the way the game works, and Lloyd doesn't have a mother, so—

DOCTOR: But Pooty is the wife and you are not a member of the family at all, unless we say that you are the adopted child.

RACHEL: Right. But Pooty's deaf. I mean, she's not, but it was just easier to make her seem like a mother since she wouldn't have to talk and she's in a wheelchair. And it worked. I mean, we won the money and Lloyd paid back his ex-wife, so . . .

DOCTOR: I know you haven't wanted to talk about your parents, Rachel, and we agreed you don't have to until you feel you're ready. The loss of our parents is the greatest single trauma of our adult lives. But I also believe that our dreams are a way of telling ourselves what we think we mustn't know, our secret wishes and fears, written in code, but the secret is there.

RACHEL: Like an anagram.

DOCTOR: Right. *(Pause)* Why do you think you picked *Your Mother or Your Wife?*

RACHEL: Oh, they picked us. I mean, we just sent in the post-card.

DOCTOR: Whose dream are we discussing?

RACHEL: Nobody's. I'm sorry I didn't say that before. I thought that was part of the therapy, to talk about everything like it was a dream. It's not a dream. I'm sorry, I was confused. Sorry.

(Pause.)

DOCTOR: Would you like to see another therapist?

RACHEL: No.

DOCTOR: Is that what you're telling me?

RACHEL: Not at all.

DOCTOR: There's nothing shameful in that. I won't be angry with you. Sometimes it's a good idea to shop around, try different types of therapies.

RACHEL: I know.

DOCTOR: I honestly think it's time, Rachel, that you try to think about what it is in the loss of your parents that is so difficult to share with me.

(Pause.)

RACHEL: My mother was run over by a school bus when I was six. My father died of a heart attack the year I married Tom.

DOCTOR: Thank you, Rachel. *(Pause)* Rachel? Did you ever wish—not really mean it—just wish that your mother would go away? Did you think that you were responsible for what happened?

RACHEL: She was run over by a school bus.

DOCTOR: And then what happened?

RACHEL: I lived with my father.

DOCTOR: Until you were how old?

RACHEL: Nineteen.

DOCTOR: And then?

RACHEL: I married Tom.

DOCTOR: And your father died.

RACHEL: Of a heart attack.

DOCTOR: What is a heart attack? Isn't it a broken heart?

SCENE 14

Living room. Lloyd and Pooty are dressed as Santa and a reindeer.

LLOYD: Ho, ho, ho!

RACHEL: Wait. Okay. Before we open presents—I love it!—I just want to say something, both of you. A year ago when I first came here and you both took me in . . . that was probably the nicest thing anybody ever did for me. You've taught me the true spirit of giving and Christmas; you've made me part of your family, you know? And . . . you're just the best family that anybody could ever ask for.

(Doorbell.)

LLOYD: Aw, who the hell is that?

(Lloyd opens the door. Tom stands there, holding a bottle of champagne and a large gift box.)

TOM: Is Rachel Fitsimmons here?
LLOYD: No, I'm sorry, there's no one here by that—
TOM: Rachel? It's Tom.
RACHEL: Oh, hi, how've you been?
TOM: May I come in?
RACHEL: Sure. Oh sure. Lloyd, Tom—Tom, Lloyd.
LLOYD: How do you do.
RACHEL: Lloyd, Pooty—Pooty . . . Tom.
TOM *(Indicating the champagne)*: This was, um, I found this sitting on the step. It says, "From Santa."
RACHEL: Uh-huh.
TOM: Nice to meet you all.
RACHEL: Pooty is deaf. And Tom is my husband.
TOM: How've you been, Rache?
RACHEL: Great. You?
TOM: I saw you on TV.
RACHEL: Uh-huh.
TOM: I almost didn't recognize you.
RACHEL: Oh.
TOM: You had a . . .
RACHEL: Planet.

TOM: On your . . .

RACHEL: Face.

TOM: Right. I thought maybe you'd remarried.

RACHEL: No.

TOM: That was . . .

RACHEL: Pretend.

TOM: TV. Right. *(Pause. He indicates gift box)* I brought you something.

RACHEL: Oh.

TOM: It's something you've always wanted. And I'm sorry I didn't give it to you before. There isn't anything I can say, Rache. I keep trying to find the right words. Something that could make . . . take away . . . Take it away. It. There, you see, all I have to do is say it and there it is. What I did. The thing I can't ever take back. It. I can't live without you, Rache. And I can't live with—with it. I can't, but I'm just so afraid to die, Rachel, I'm afraid.

RACHEL: No one's going to die.

TOM: Well, we're all going to die.

RACHEL: Not right now, please.

TOM: I'm so sorry, Rachel.

RACHEL: Why don't we have some of this champagne? Lloyd, would you get some glasses, please?

(Lloyd goes off.)

Oh Tom, it was very nice of you to bring the champagne, that means a lot to me.

TOM: It was just sitting on the step.

RACHEL: Oh, well, it was nice of someone then, wasn't it? *(The gift box)* What's this? Is this for me?

TOM: Uh-huh.

RACHEL: You brought this? I can't think what it could be . . . Does anybody mind?

(Pooty signs. Rachel unwraps the package.)

TOM: The boys said if I brought you that maybe you'd come home. They're with Jeanette and Freddie for the weekend.

RACHEL: Oh, how is Jeanette?

TOM: Everybody sends their love. We all miss you.

RACHEL *(Looks in the box)*: Tom!

TOM: You like him?

RACHEL: Oh, he's so sweet.

TOM: You can name him whatever you want.

RACHEL: He's so beautiful. Look! Tom, thank you. *(She holds up a stuffed animal puppy)*

TOM: And you don't have to clean up after him.

RACHEL: I know. Look everybody!

LLOYD *(Returns with the champagne and a glass of milk for himself; he pours)*: Cute.

RACHEL: Oh, thank you.

TOM: You're welcome.

LLOYD: How 'bout some champagne? Everybody like champagne? Poot? *(Hands them their glasses)*

TOM: Thanks.

RACHEL: Awww.

LLOYD: Drink up.

TOM: Please come home, Rache. We miss you.

RACHEL: Cheers! *(She clinks her glass against Tom's, overemphatically, and her glass shatters)* Whoops! Oh God.

LLOYD: That's okay, I'll get you another one.

RACHEL: Thanks.

(Lloyd goes off.)

(To Tom and Pooty) Oh, go ahead, please. I'm fine.

TOM *(To Pooty)*: Cheers.

(Pooty signs the word for "cheers." She and Tom drink. Lloyd returns with another glass and pours.)

LLOYD: Here you go.

RACHEL: Thank you, Lloyd. Cheers.

(Tom bends forward in sudden discomfort. Pooty emits a small noise.)

TOM: Is there a bathroom?
LLOYD: Poot?

(Rachel holds her glass, untasted, watching as Tom and Pooty double over in pain.)

TOM: Ow!
POOTY: Lloyd!

(Lloyd is stunned.)

TOM: Jesus! Aaaagh!
POOTY: Lloyd!
TOM: Aaaaaaa!
POOTY: AAAAAAAAAAAAAAAAAA!

(Tom and Pooty die.)

SCENE 15

The car. Rachel drives. Lloyd in his Santa suit.

RACHEL: Calm . . . Calm . . . Okay. Did I miss my exit? Okay. Lloyd? Okay. Okay, if we call the police—did we? Are we calling the police? Did we? No, I remember, okay. We could. Here's the thing: we didn't. We called the ambulance, okay. Why didn't we call the police? Because. They'll think we did it. Why will they think we did it? Because we didn't call the police. No, our fingerprints were on the bottle. "So what?" "What do you mean 'so what?' Why did you leave your family? Why do you have assumed names? What are you hiding?" "Nothing." "Uh-huh. Where'd you get all this cash in hundred-dollar-bills?" "Oh, we won it on a game show." "What game show?" "*Your Mother or Your Wife.*" "Is this your mother?" "No." "Is this your wife?" "No." Turnpike! . . . Is this the right ramp? Lloyd? *(Looks in rearview mirror)* I think those people are following me. Are those the same people? No, wait, Tom brought the champagne! That's right. Tom brought the champagne. "We're all going to die," remember? *(She reads a road sign)* West. We're all going to die. Just take a look over your shoulder and tell me if those are the same people . . . No! No, it was sitting on the step, that's right, remember? From Santa. Or he was lying. All right, wait. Wait. Maybe it was just a bad bottle. Maybe—maybe—they're following me. Don't turn around. Look like you're having a good time. Uh-huh! Uh-huh! Really! . . . Oh God.

(Rachel turns on the radio.)

ANNOUNCER: The mellow sound of Nat King Cole. Gone before his time. It's ten A.M. Christmas morning. Let's hope Santa left something special under your tree. In the news—

(Rachel turns off the radio.)

RACHEL: Wait a minute! Santa! Santa. Sat—na. At—sna. At—san. Tas—na. As—nat. Santa, Merry Christmas from Santa . . . Sat—an. Satin. Satin. *Satan!* Merry Christmas from Satan! Oh God. Christ's birthday, Merry Christmas from Satan, Lloyd! That's horrible. Why is this happening? Why is it always Christmas? I love Christmas. I always used to say I wanted to live in Alaska because they had snow all year round and Santa was up there, so it must always be Christmas . . . Oh, Lloyd. They won't feel any more pain from now on, I know they won't. No more pain from now on, all right, Santa Claus? I'll drink to that.

SCENE 16

Night. Snow. Rachel is still driving. Lloyd in his suit, staring.

RACHEL: Toopy . . . P . . . Oop. Oopy. Toopy. Poot. Pyoot. Ypoot. Ytpoo. It. It . . . Toopy. Two Ps. Two . . . Y-po-to. Toy—po. Poy sounds like boy. Two boys! I have two boys. *(Pause)* I don't even know what state we're in, do you? *(Sees road sign)* Wait, can you read that? . . . Spring . . . *field*. Springfield!?!? Is that what it said? How can we be back in Springfield— *(Reads)* Ohio! Springfield, Ohio, thank you, God! Springfield, Ohio . . . *(Sighs with relief)* Oh God. Who would ever want to live in Springfield, Ohio? *(She has a revelation)* Nobody.

SCENE 17

A seedy hotel room; Lloyd remains in his Santa suit.

RACHEL: Lloyd, I know we can be happy here, I just know we can. Who would ever think to look for us in Springfield, Ohio! Nobody. Why would we ever want to go back to Springfield? We wouldn't, you see, we wouldn't! And the lady at the real estate agency said there's one in every state. Fifty Springfields. So we don't have to stay here if we don't like it. We don't have to do anything. We can go anywhere, we can be any-body. We can go from Springfield to Springfield. How many people ever get the chance to do that in their whole lives? . . . Lloyd . . . I know I can't take her place. But she'll always be right here. You're what keeps her memory alive. But you have to keep yourself alive. You have to *eat* something. And we have to get you out of that suit. We're lucky to be alive, I mean, we could have had some of that champagne. Well, you don't drink, but . . . Let's pick names. What do you like? How about

Jessie? I'll be Jessie or you be Jesse and I'll be Mrs. Mancini. I can find a new doctor. You know, it's a good idea to shop around, try different types of therapies—

LLOYD: SHUT UP! SHUT THE FUCK UP PLEASE! COULD WE HAVE ONE—TINY—MOMENT OF SILENCE IF IT ISN'T TOO MUCH TO ASK FOR? PLEASE?

(Pause.)

RACHEL: I'm sorry.
LLOYD: What?
RACHEL: I said I'm sorry.
LLOYD: I can't hear you.

(Pause.)

RACHEL: I said . . .

(Pause. Rachel signs "I'm sorry.")

SCENE 18

Another doctor's office.

SECOND DOCTOR: Do you have nightmares, Mrs. Mancini?
RACHEL: No.
SECOND DOCTOR: Phobias?
RACHEL: No.
SECOND DOCTOR: Eczema? Asthma?
RACHEL: No.
SECOND DOCTOR: Do you take drugs?
RACHEL: No.
SECOND DOCTOR: Alcohol?
RACHEL: No.
SECOND DOCTOR: Are you an alcoholic?
RACHEL: No.

SECOND DOCTOR: Would you say you're chronically depressed?

RACHEL: No.

SECOND DOCTOR: Or unfulfilled in some way?

RACHEL: No.

SECOND DOCTOR: Have you ever tried to kill yourself?

RACHEL: No.

SECOND DOCTOR: Is it difficult for you to make a decision?

RACHEL: No.

SECOND DOCTOR: Are you sure?

RACHEL: Mm-hm.

SECOND DOCTOR: Do you have trouble sleeping?

RACHEL: No.

SECOND DOCTOR: You sleep too much?

RACHEL: No.

SECOND DOCTOR: Dietary difficulties?

RACHEL: No.

SECOND DOCTOR: Overeating?

RACHEL: No.

SECOND DOCTOR: Undereating?

RACHEL: No.

SECOND DOCTOR: Is sex a problem for you, Mrs. Mancini?

RACHEL: No.

SECOND DOCTOR: Does that embarrass you, my asking?

RACHEL: No.

SECOND DOCTOR: Do you ever have any trouble relating to new people?

RACHEL: No.

SECOND DOCTOR: Telling the truth?

RACHEL: No.

SECOND DOCTOR: No? . . . What's the problem?

RACHEL: My husband tried to kill me.

SECOND DOCTOR: Tried to kill you?

RACHEL: Twice.

SECOND DOCTOR: Why would he want to kill you?

RACHEL: I don't know

SECOND DOCTOR: Did you call the police?

RACHEL: No.

SECOND DOCTOR: Why didn't you call the police?

RACHEL: Because I didn't think they'd believe me.

SECOND DOCTOR: Why wouldn't they believe you?

RACHEL: Because I'd run away and changed my name and was living with another man and his wife and then when they all got poisoned . . .

SECOND DOCTOR: Who got poisoned?

RACHEL: My husband and the other man's wife. Did. Pretty much.

SCENE 19

Another hotel room.

LLOYD: You know what I feel like having?

RACHEL: What?

LLOYD: You know what I really feel like having?

RACHEL: What?

LLOYD: You know what I really feel like having right now?

RACHEL: What?

LLOYD: Champagne.

SCENE 20

Another doctor's office.

THIRD DOCTOR: You're not from Alabama.

RACHEL: No.

THIRD DOCTOR: Now how did I know that?

RACHEL: You see, two Christmases ago, my husband Tom . . . Well, we've lived in Springfield before.

THIRD DOCTOR: Oh, you have.

RACHEL: Twice. And I have two sons, too, actually. And my husband tried to kill me twice, too.

THIRD DOCTOR: Your husband? Tried—

RACHEL *(Overlapping)*: Two Ps! . . . Pooty . . . My first shrink said that Pooty was an unusual name.

THIRD DOCTOR: Oh, you've been in therapy before.

RACHEL: Twice. But . . . Okay: How long do you think a person could live if they drank nothing but champagne and they didn't eat anything? Just out of curiosity.

THIRD DOCTOR: Well . . .

RACHEL: Does a month seem like a long time? To you.

SCENE 21

Another hotel room.

LLOYD: Here's a question.

RACHEL: No.

LLOYD: Do you remember asking me if we ever really know anybody?

RACHEL: Not until you eat something.

LLOYD: You remember that?

RACHEL *(Unpacking groceries)*: Do you hear me?

LLOYD: You asked me if I thought we ever really knew anybody.

RACHEL: You are going to eat something if it kills me.

LLOYD: And I've thought about it . . . And I would have to say . . .

RACHEL: You don't have to taste it.

LLOYD: My considered opinion would be . . .

RACHEL: Just smell it.

LLOYD: No. No way.

RACHEL: Croissants, Lloyd!

LLOYD: Not on your life.

RACHEL: Look, pâté.

LLOYD: No dice.

RACHEL: Just open your mouth and take one bite.

LLOYD: Ixnay.

RACHEL: Strawberries.

LLOYD: Nope.

RACHEL: Ice cream.

LLOYD: Uh-uh.

RACHEL: It's pistachio.

LLOYD: No way, José.

RACHEL: Lloyd, you can't—

LLOYD: Forget about it.

RACHEL: Soup. Soup!

LLOYD: No chance.

RACHEL: You can't survive on champagne alone, it's an old saying.

LLOYD: No, no, a thousand times no.

RACHEL: I need you now.

LLOYD: Nyet.

RACHEL: Please.

LLOYD: Non.

RACHEL: You can't live on wine.

LLOYD: Nein!

SCENE 22

Another doctor's office.

FOURTH DOCTOR: This is very important, Cheryl. We've talked about the birth scream. It is a terrible shock to be torn away in a shower of blood with your mother screaming and your home torn open and the strange doctor with his rubber hands slapping you with all his might and the cold light piercing the dark, the warm beautiful wet dark, the silent murmuring safe dark of Mummy everywhere and Daddy, everything is one and everything is sex and we are all together for eternity and we are happy and nothing ever passes through your mind but good thoughts until suddenly this squeezing is going on around you and everyone is pushing and pulling and cold steel tongs pinch your skin and pull you by the top of your head and you don't want to go, no, you don't want to leave your home where you're always floating and your mother's heart is always beating for something unknown and cruel where people are cold and you're stinging now, everything is breaking, it makes you want to scream, Cheryl, makes you want to scream the scream of all ages, scream of the greatest tragedy of all time and your mummy is screaming and your daddy is screaming and now all the doctors are screaming and everything's blinding you and you're torn away and they're hitting you and they throw you up in the air and you open your eyes and your mother is covered in blood and you scream, Cheryl, scream, scream, *scream*, Cheryl, SCREAM, *SCREAM*!!!

(Pause) All right, we'll try it again.

SCENE 23

Another doctor's office and another hotel room.

LLOYD: Not all champagne is champagne. They call it champagne. Sure, they call it champagne. I'll tell you what is interesting about champagne. Pain. It is painstakingly made. They take great pains.

FIFTH DOCTOR: Say I am a decent human being.

RACHEL: I am a decent human being.

FIFTH DOCTOR: Say I deserve to be loved.

RACHEL: I deserve to be loved.

FIFTH DOCTOR: Now repeat everything after me. I was put on this earth to love and be loved.

LLOYD: Great pains, believe me.

FIFTH DOCTOR: I was put on this earth . . .

RACHEL: I was put on this earth to love and be loved . . .

FIFTH DOCTOR: I am whole when I am alone and I am part of everything.

LLOYD *(Overlapping)*: And it is only in the region of Champagne where champagne is made.

FIFTH DOCTOR: Mrs. Bophtelophti? . . . I said I am whole when I'm alone and I am part of everything.

RACHEL: Uh-huh.

FIFTH DOCTOR: And I would like you to repeat that.

RACHEL: Wait a minute.

FIFTH DOCTOR: What?

RACHEL: Wait a minute!

FIFTH DOCTOR: What?

RACHEL: You know what? Things just happen. People die. And bus drivers don't always look where they're going, even if they should, even if they're driving a school bus. Even if you love somebody they can still take a contract out on your life. And if you try to help somebody because they've been kind to you when you needed them, they can *still* refuse to eat and drink nothing but champagne, cham*pagne*, that's all they'll drink, and if you ask them to please, *please* take off their Santa Claus suit, just when they go out, just when you go to the store, they won't. So? Things just happen!

SCENE 24

Another hotel room. Lloyd moans in the glow of the television.

RACHEL: I'm here. Shhhh. I'm here, here we go. Mother's milk. *(Produces two bottles of champagne)* It's your Christmas present, right? I couldn't think what else to get you. I'm sorry. I got you two bottles. We're going to have a festive Christmas, just the two of us. It's our anniversary, too, remember? Don't you want to listen to the news? . . . Where's the knob? Did you pull out the knob?

(Rachel takes the knob from Lloyd. He tries to remove a champagne cork, but is too weak.)

It's the one night in the year they save up all the good news. Don't you want to hear it? I'll help you with that, just a sec. Look. Doesn't that woman look like Trish Whatshername from Hands Across the Sea. Hammers. *(Putting in the knob)* My God! Lloyd, look!

(Sound comes on.)

ANNOUNCER: . . . refused to comment, but local spokesmen say Ms. Hammers may have embezzled as much as a half a million dollars in her more than twenty years as an accountant for the humanitarian organization.

RACHEL *(Under)*: Oh my . . .

ANNOUNCER: David Harbinger spoke with Roy Morgrebi, president of the northeast chapter of Hands Across the Sea in Springfield.

RACHEL: There's Roy! Lloyd!

ROY: It just boggles the mind, you know. Very sweet girl.

SECOND ANNOUNCER: Would you say this is something we should all begin to be wary of? Donating money to charity—

ROY: No.

SECOND ANNOUNCER: —which will end up somehow in private hands?

ROY: Definitely not. I feel this is an isolated case, one hopes, and obviously we intend to institute tighter controls.

FIRST ANNOUNCER: Police are still looking for the two alleged accomplices in last year's Christmas killing here in Springfield. More news after this word.

RACHEL *(Over the fading sound of a commercial)*: They think we did it! Lloyd! They think we did it . . . She tried to poison us! And it wasn't Tom! It wasn't Tom at all! . . . Lloyd, we've got to go to the police, because WE DIDN'T DO IT! Don't you see? Okay! Okay! Say good-bye to Springfield!

(Lloyd is dead.)

Say good-bye . . .

(Lloyd slumps forward. Rachel grabs him by the shirt, shakes him, lets him fall.)

SCENE 25

A shelter. Rachel, the Sixth Doctor and two Derelicts in front of the television.

TV ANNOUNCER: Street people they're called and Anne Lacher-Holden has the story.

FIRST DERELICT *(Overlapping)*: Shit on the floor, shit on the floor and you know it!

SIXTH DOCTOR *(Overlapping)*: This is us, don't you want to listen?

WOMAN ANNOUNCER: In the summertime they seem to be everywhere, but where do they go in the winter? It is in shelters like this one, in storefronts all over the city where the needy, the cold and hungry, come for food and comfort. How many of these people would starve to death if not for the efforts and dedication of individuals like Dr. Mahalia Maden.

SECOND DERELICT: Dr. M&M's!

WOMAN ANNOUNCER: Doctor, how many years have you been running this shelter?

SIXTH DOCTOR'S VOICE: Six years this Christmas, Anne.

WOMAN ANNOUNCER: And where do you get your funds?

SECOND DERELICT *(Under)*: Steal it.

SIXTH DOCTOR'S VOICE: Well, money's a funny thing, you know. A lot of people want to help save the whales, but tell them they can help save a human being . . .

WOMAN ANNOUNCER: That's right. What kind of people stay here and where do they come from?

SIXTH DOCTOR'S VOICE: All over. We have bank presidents, writers, you name it.

WOMAN ANNOUNCER: What brings them here?

SIXTH DOCTOR'S VOICE: Life's been reckless with these people, Anne. Some more than others. Often they carry no identification whatsoever, it's difficult.

WOMAN ANNOUNCER: I see.

SIXTH DOCTOR'S VOICE: We have one of our people, I guess you could say she's our mascot. She came to us our first night six years ago on Christmas Eve—no idea who she was, no name, we thought she was deaf. I'll be darned if a few weeks ago she didn't start to talk in her sleep. Talks a blue streak.

WOMAN ANNOUNCER: Really?

SIXTH DOCTOR'S VOICE: Who's to say these people can't lead normal, healthy lives again.

WOMAN ANNOUNCER: You say they can. Doctor, it's been a pleasure talking with you. I'm Anne Lacher-Holden with *Street Beat*.

SECOND DERELICT: I'm bored.

ANNOUNCER: Thank you, Anne. Coming up we'll take a look at a woman who claims she's Santa Claus. And Marge von Bargen will—

(Sixth Doctor switches off the television.)

FIRST DERELICT: Shit on your floor and you know it!

(Derelicts disperse.)

SIXTH DOCTOR *(To Rachel)*: No more secrets now, Eve. The whole world knows you can hear me and you know you hear me, because you spoke to me last night. Look at me: I asked you what was wrong and you said you were afraid and you were not asleep, Eve, so don't try that with me now. Your eyes were open and you answered me. Look at me: You answered me. What did you say? Everyone's afraid, Eve, I'm afraid. What did you say? A man in a ski mask who follows you when you leave here. Why does he follow you? Whose face is he hiding,

Eve? Whose face? Behind the mask . . . I have bad dreams too, Eve. I wake up in the middle of the night, too, and want someone to hold me. I remember what I did to someone once and can never, never undo. Because you can never give back a life. But I made a pledge to myself that I would try. And I went to school and I studied to be a doctor and I swore to myself that I would scrimp and save and deny myself and do anything, Eve, if I could give one person back their life. And six years ago on Christmas Eve we opened the doors here. Who do you think was the first person to walk in off the street and join us? Eve . . . Do you want to know my dream? That someday you'll trust me. And tell me all your dreams, all the good ones, so I can help you make them all come true. That's my dream . . . The TV people gave me some tickets to a talk show. Would you like that? A talk show? How does that sound?

SCENE 26

HOST: And we're back with the author of *Unrepentant Killer.* Sue, if you hadn't been acquitted, do you think you'd still feel this same sense of—

SUE: Yes—

HOST: —purpose.

SUE: My husband was able to terrorize me and—

HOST: Uh-huh.

SUE: —my kids because we were too frightened he might hurt *us.* But our rage was there, believe me.

HOST: As was borne out by your—subsequen— . . .

SUE *(Overlapping)*: Look out here at all these faces: these people are all potential killers—again, I'm not recommending they do what I did.

HOST: Perhaps you wouldn't have had to—

SUE: That's right.

HOST: —if you felt—

SUE *(Overlapping slightly)*: *Experienced* my own fury, yes.

HOST *(Overlapping)*: Yes. Right.

SUE: Here, see, now this right here is a perfect example of what I call the I-Am-Unworthy-Please-Oh-Who?-Me?-I-Wouldn't-Hurt-A-Fly type.

(Sue approaches the front row of the audience. Monitors reveal Rachel and Sixth Doctor, seated. Sue addresses Rachel.)

Stand up, please.

SIXTH DOCTOR: No, she can't really—

SUE: Yes, she can, give her some credit—come.

SIXTH DOCTOR: No, really—

SUE *(To Rachel as she drags her center)*: I bet I know who you'd like to kill already. *(Turns Rachel to face the audience)* There. Now isn't she lovely? *(Applause)* Pick a face out there and imagine firing a bullet right between their eyes. Anyone. Bam! Right between their beady little slits . . . *(Rachel stares out blankly)* See? She's terrified someone's going to hurt *her*. *(To Rachel)* This time you're going to get *them*. Say: "I am a cold-blooded killer. I—" What's your name? *(Rachel sees something in the audience)* Do you have a name?

RACHEL: No.

SIXTH DOCTOR: Good, Eve!

SUE: Eve, okay.

RACHEL: No.

SUE: "I, Eve, am a cold-blooded—"

RACHEL *(Overlapping "I, Eve—")*: NOOOOOOOO!

(At the same time, a Man in a ski mask has screamed from the aisle in the theatre.)

MAN: DEVIL WOMAN! *(He rushes the stage, pointing a handgun at Rachel)*

HOST: Look out! Somebody!

(The gun goes off. Rachel ducks and Sue, author of Unrepentant Killer, *is mortally wounded. Pandemonium.)*

Look out! My god! Doctor! DOCTOR!
RACHEL: NO! NO! NO! NO!

(The Host and Sue disappear. The Sixth Doctor has rushed to Rachel's side.)

SCENE 27

The action is continuous. Rachel repeats the word "no" over and over again, struggling to break free from the Sixth Doctor.

SIXTH DOCTOR: Yes! Yes, Eve, yes! Yes! Look at me, yes, you spoke, yes, yes, yes. You spoke. Look at me. You spoke. Eve, yes, say yes. Say yes. Shhhh, I'm here, close your eyes, I'm here, yes, you spoke. Yes, and I was wrong. There was a man. You were so right, there was a man and I was wrong, I'm sorry, Eve, I was wrong. There was a man and he was trying to hurt you, but he's gone now. *(Rachel has quieted down)* We'll never know why he was trying to hurt you. The important thing is you spoke out loud and people heard you and I heard you and *you* heard you, Eve. You heard you. You. Eve. If you can tell yourself what you want, you can have it. I swear to you. I used to drive a school bus. Did you know that? I drove a school bus. And how many bus drivers do you think become doctors, Eve? None. Not at all. *Except the ones who do.* All right, Eve, close your eyes. I want you to imagine a place. I want you to imagine the most beautiful place in all the world. I don't want you to think about what anybody said you could or couldn't do. I want you to dream, Eve. I want you to imagine a time of year—your favorite time of year, the weather that gives you goosebumps—the right temperature, the right light in the sky, the right smell in the air. I want you to imagine someone standing there, Eve. Someone who makes people feel good about themselves and does all the things you ever wanted to do and has all the things you ever wanted to have. I want you to imagine that person standing there in that place at that exact time of day doing exactly what that person would be doing . . . Eve . . . if that person . . .

SCENE 28

An office.

RACHEL: Yes?

WOMAN PATIENT: That's the end.

RACHEL: You wake up?

WOMAN PATIENT: I wake up.

RACHEL: And how do you feel?

WOMAN PATIENT: Happy.

RACHEL: The dream makes you feel happy?

WOMAN PATIENT: Yes.

RACHEL: I'm afraid we're going to have to stop here, Sharon.

WOMAN PATIENT: But what does it mean?

RACHEL: What does it mean?

WOMAN PATIENT: Why am I happy?

RACHEL: Does there have to be a reason?

WOMAN PATIENT: I don't know.

RACHEL: You're happy.

WOMAN PATIENT: Yes.

RACHEL: You feel happy now?

WOMAN PATIENT: Yes. Oh. That's what it means. It means I'm happy.

RACHEL: Yes.

WOMAN PATIENT: It means I'm happy.

RACHEL: It could mean that.

WOMAN PATIENT: It means I'm happy. Thank you.

RACHEL: Don't thank me, thank yourself.

WOMAN PATIENT *(With Rachel)*: "Thank yourself." Well . . . Merry Christmas.

RACHEL: You too, Sharon.

WOMAN PATIENT: I'll see you next week. *(She leaves)*

RECEPTIONIST *(Pokes her head in)*: Doctor, there's a student here from the University of Alaska waiting to see you. They called while you were in your session to say he was coming over.

RACHEL: Send him in, thanks.

RECEPTIONIST *(To the offstage student)*: You can go on in. There you go.

(She exits as Tom Jr. enters.)

TOM JR.: Doctor?

RACHEL: Yes, I'm— *(Her throat catches)* Sorry, there's something caught in my throat. I'm sorry if I kept you waiting.

TOM JR. *(Extending his hand)*: Tom Fitsimmons.

RACHEL: Tom. Won't you, please . . . Have a seat, Tom. Please. Anywhere.

(Tom sits in the only chair.)

What's the problem? What can I do for you? Take your time, relax, Tom, what's the story?

TOM JR.: I, uh . . . I was just trying to get some sleeping pills and they said I would have to, uh . . .

RACHEL: I see.

TOM JR.: You look really familiar.

RACHEL: I do?

TOM JR.: You look really familiar. Where do I know you from? . . .

RACHEL: Why do you think you're having trouble sleeping, Tom? Are you? Having trouble?

TOM JR.: I know who you look like.

RACHEL: Your mother.

TOM JR.: Yes.

RACHEL: That's the transference, Tom. The patient projects an image onto the parent. Onto the . . .

TOM JR.: It's incredible.

RACHEL: But you say you feel you need something, is that right?

TOM JR.: No, but like I've only seen pictures of her, but you really do. I mean, you're a lot older.

RACHEL: Of course.

TOM JR.: But still, I mean, it's . . . incredible.

RACHEL: Good . . . Tom, what is all this about sleeping pills? Is that what you need?

TOM JR.: Sort of.

RACHEL: Why?

TOM JR.: I can't sleep. But I mean, it's just for this week. I mean, next week I'll be fine, so it doesn't have to be very many.

RACHEL: Why is it just this week?

TOM JR.: Because.

RACHEL: Does it have something to do with Christmas? . . .

TOM JR.: You know, I really feel better now that we've talked. I really do. I don't think I need sleeping pills at all, it's incredible, thank you.

RACHEL: Sit down.

TOM JR.: I'm serious.

RACHEL: Sit down, Tom. What is it about Christmas? . . . Some people think that the things you're afraid to think about are the things which eventually destroy you. And that if you talk about them, as painful as that is, it helps them to go away.

TOM JR.: I'm not afraid to think about them.

RACHEL: Then what is it? You think I won't believe you?

TOM JR.: Maybe.

RACHEL: Why don't you try me?

TOM JR.: My mother . . . the one . . .

RACHEL: Right.

TOM JR.: Ran away like on Christmas.

RACHEL: How old were you?

TOM JR.: Four.

RACHEL: Go on.

TOM JR.: So the next year our father, you know, leaves us with friends, so—he says because he's going to bring our mother back, because . . . I don't know.

RACHEL: You have brothers and sisters?

TOM JR.: One brother. Younger. And instead he gets killed.

RACHEL: Your—?

TOM JR.: Father. By . . . well, it probably had something to do . . .

RACHEL: I'm listening.

TOM JR.: It may have had something to do with this whole . . . scandal. Anyway, he died. And they said our mother was involved, but they never were able to find her. And so we were raised, you know, by—my brother and I— by these neighbors and they were really nice. And then . . . my brother disappeared when he was twelve and we didn't hear anything for a long time. And then he called and said he's found this woman in California and she was gonna pay or something and . . . I guess he just freaked out and he shot this lady on some talk show right around Christmastime . . . I don't know. I mean, they didn't convict him, but . . . I kind of thought I'd get away, you know? Alaska seemed like the place.

RACHEL: It is.

TOM JR.: Not really. They have Christmas here too.

RACHEL: You have no memories of your mother, Tom?

TOM JR.: No. Oh, yes, I do—one. But I mean, I think I dreamed it. I mean, I don't know. I think I dreamed it.

RACHEL: What is the memory?

TOM JR.: Well, it's Christmas.

RACHEL: Uh-huh.

TOM JR.: And, um, she's like reaching up, putting something up.

RACHEL: On the tree.

TOM JR.: Uh-huh. Or something. And she's really . . . she's really happy. Everything's bright and she's all in a glow and she looks right at me and says, "How's that?"

RACHEL: "How's that?"

TOM JR.: Like that. And I don't know. I just said it, you know?

RACHEL: What?

TOM JR.: Lousy, you're fired. I was just kidding.

RACHEL: Of course.

TOM JR.: But . . . sometimes it seems like that was the start of everything. It's like I hurt her feelings or something and she left and my father left and my brother left . . . I keep feeling like if I could just go back to that—time. And she would turn to me, you know, all lit up and say, "How's that?" I'd say, "Beautiful, Mom." You know.

RACHEL: Uh-huh.

TOM JR.: Because it was like for one second I wanted to spoil everything. Everybody was too happy and I was too excited. But I would take it back. I would take it all back, because I didn't mean it.

RACHEL: Of course you didn't mean it.

TOM JR.: No, but I can't. It's like I can't wake up. I just know—I feel if I could just wake up, we'd all be there around the tree and my mom and my dad would take care of me. And I keep pinching myself and pinching . . .

RACHEL: Trying to wake up.

TOM JR.: Yes. I just keep wishing—

RACHEL: Yes.

TOM JR.: —for . . .

RACHEL: Someplace where it's always Christmas.

TOM JR.: Yes. How do you know? . . . Oh, I see, now you become my mother.

RACHEL: How's this time for you, Tom? Is this all right?

TOM JR.: Fine. Are we through?

RACHEL: Tomorrow at this time?

TOM JR.: Fine.

RACHEL: And the day after?

TOM JR.: Great. Wait, that's Christmas.

RACHEL: Would you rather not?

TOM JR.: No. You work on Christmas?

RACHEL: I love my work. And try to hold off the sleeping pills for a while, all right?

TOM JR.: Sure.

RACHEL: Tomorrow then?

TOM JR.: Great.

RACHEL: Tom? . . . I'm sorry I kept you waiting.

TOM JR.: Oh, no problem. Oh, I see. Right. Right. Well . . .
Tomorrow.

*(Tom Jr. goes. Rachel moves to the window as "I'll Be
Home for Christmas" plays and snow falls. Lights fade.)*

END OF PLAY

BLUE WINDOW

— For Dr. Tim —

Blue Window was first presented by The Production Company (Norman René, Artistic Director; Abigail Franklin, Managing Director) at Theatre Guinevere in New York City on May 28, 1984. The production was directed by Norman René, with sets by Loy Arcenas, costumes by Walker Hicklin and lighting by Debra J. Kletter. The cast was as follows:

EMILY	Maureen Silliman
TOM	Lawrence Joshua
LIBBY	Randy Danson
NORBERT	Matt Craven
BOO	Christine Estabrook
GRIEVER	Brad O'Hare
ALICE	Margo Skinner

The following year René staged *Blue Window* at New Haven's Long Wharf Theatre and Costa Mesa's South Coast Repertory; the South Coast production went on to a commercial run at the New Mayfair Theatre in Santa Monica.

Blue Window won the first George and Elisabeth Marton Award, a Los Angeles Drama Critics' Award and a Drama-Logue Award. It was televised on *American Playhouse* in 1987.

The floor, walls and upstage scrim are all a light blue. Five open doorways stage left. Black, sculptural shapes flecked with bright confetti markings represent furniture. Down right is Libby's bar unit. Up right, Alice and Boo's sofa unit. Center, Tom and Emily's ottoman. Up left, Norbert's armchair. Down left, Griever's dressing unit and mirror. Upstage, slightly tilted toward the audience, hangs a large transparent canvas, framed like a window, splattered with bright paint. Several smaller units hold flowers and phones. The feeling is open and attractive; only a little sterile.

As stage directions suggest, dialogue often overlaps, but is printed here consecutively for ease in reading. Two or more conversations may be taking place simultaneously; two, three or even four characters may speak at once. The effect desired is verbal music, with main themes and counterpoint or accompaniment. Those interested in producing the play should consult the acting edition, in which parallel columns are used.

LANGUAGE TAPE VOICE *(In the darkness)*: Uno, due, tre, quat-
tro, cinque, sei, sette . . .

*Lights up slowly. Birds; traffic. Emily stands alone. She is
dressed for a cool day. She unwraps and chews a piece of
gum. Tom enters with sheet music, pencil, beer. In fits and
starts, we hear the song he is trying to write. He makes a
correction in the music and we hear the altered melody.
Emily crosses upstage behind the canvas, visible through
the splashes of paint.*

    *Libby enters in her raincoat, glasses, rainbonnet, black
scarf. She has a bag of groceries, her handbag, her keys in
her mouth and cigarette in hand. The keys go into the
handbag, the cigarette into her mouth. She sets the groceries
down and takes her coat off, revealing a slip underneath.
She exits on classical music, which brings on Norbert in
exercise outfit, carrying an orange and a record jacket.
Libby reenters with two lists—To Do and To Buy—which
she tacks up on the wall. Norbert begins to assemble a jig-*

saw puzzle, seated on the back of his chair, puzzle in lap. Typing from offstage. Libby exits.

Boo enters with a small, dying plant which she places by the big canvas. She talks to the plant in hushed tones of affection. Bored, she sits and listens to a language tape, quickly losing interest. Libby reenters with a kitchen timer which she is winding; she now wears a loose, flowing kimono. Boo changes the tape on her Walkman. Libby goes off and comes back, looking for the handbag which is under her arm. Boo jogs to music which we do not hear. Discouraged at the size of her thighs, she tosses off the headphones and exits as Griever, in his bathrobe, enters: dance music. He checks himself in mirror, lays out new clothes. Boo reenters with cigarette and ashtray. Libby has gone and come again, this time with a bowl of mussels and knife, trying hopelessly to open the shells. Griever has gone off and returned with shoes. The music gets to him and he dances around the stage into each of the other characters' territories, finally exiting to take a shower; music fades.

Tom picks up guitar, plays first part of his song. Typing from off. Typing stops. By now Libby has cut her finger and gone off for a Band-Aid. Boo, unable to find a single matchbook with a match in it, has tossed her last cigarette across the room; she finally finds a match, retrieves cigarette, lights it and walks several times around her sofa as if she might get somewhere, eventually. Norbert has peeled his orange, eaten it, and is still assembling his puzzle. Emily has crossed further left behind the painting.

TOM *(To someone offstage)*: Do you like this? It should like . . . I like the fact that it doesn't go anywhere. I mean, I can hear the whole thing. Like I did this and I did this and then this happened and this happened and so what? It should be kind of bland, you know, and flat out . . .

(Libby comes on with seven place cards.)

Do you know anybody who writes lyrics? I mean, I don't even think I would want it to rhyme. And the voice should have the melody without any beefing up, it should be thin, and the guitar stays constant. Like just one awful thing after another. I can hear it . . . I just can't . . .

LIBBY *(Going through place cards, unable to assign the last card a name)*: Alice, Boo, Emily, Tom . . . Norbert. Alice, Boo, Emily, Tom, Norbert . . . Griever.

TOM: Like I went here and I did this and I did this and I went here and I did this and I did this . . .

LIBBY *(Overlapping)*: Alice, Boo, Emily . . . Tom . . . Alice, Boo, Emily . . . LIBBY! Libby, Libby, Libby, Libby . . .

TOM: Maybe it'd sound better on a piano. God, I used to have this beautiful, beautiful piano, real nice touch, baby grand . . . You know who got it. "The kids'll want to take piano lessons . . . Get your own piano." Duh, it is my own piano. Nobody's going to take piano lessons, I can guarantee . . .

(Libby exits.)

I just don't want this to sound like a folk song . . .

ALICE *(Entering, high from her work)*: "Moonlight and love songs never out of date / Hearts full of passion, jealousy and hate—"

(Kisses Boo on the top of her head; Boo is again listening to her language tape.)

What are we listening to? "Woman needs man!"

BOO: What?

ALICE: Eye-talian?

BOO: Si.

ALICE: Are we bringing wine or flowers or what?

BOO: Never on Sunday, remember? It's Sunday.

ALICE: We didn't drink the whole case, did we? What do you mean "we," white man?

(Libby reenters with cookbook, phone and hammer; she dials)

BOO: Breakthrough?

(Griever's phone rings.)

ALICE: I don't know, maybe. Maybe not.

(Boo returns to her tape.)

I can take the hint, never mind.
BOO: What?
ALICE *(Exiting)*: Niente. Impari il tuo Italiano.

(Griever rushes on, dripping wet, with towel, answers the phone.)

GRIEVER: I'm coming. I've got my coat on.
LIBBY: Did you ever do mussels?
GRIEVER: I'm not sure I know what you mean.
LIBBY: Never mind, Griever, never mind, here it is, they steam themselves open, good-bye. *(She hangs up)*
GRIEVER: Good-bye to you. *(Into mirror)* And you and you. And allllllll the little people. The little tiny Irish people.

(Libby exits.)

Good-bye, good-byyyyyyeee. Auf wiedersehen. Good night. We hate to say good-bye. We hate to see you leave, but get out. Go home, go home, a dog with his bone. I am so embarrassed for you. *(Puts on pants)* I am so embarrassed for your family. I am so embarrassed for the children and their queen. Debbie. *(Belt)*
ALICE *(Back on)*: Kiss me.
GRIEVER: Queen Debbie.
BOO: What?
GRIEVER: Debbie the queen of the debutantes.

ALICE: Kiss me.

BOO: I can't, my mother is at the airport. "La mia mama e all'aeroporto."

ALICE: Really. Uh-huh. *(Taking both sides of an imaginary conversation)* "Marry me." "I can't, my umbrella is in the kitchen." "Then run away with me."

BOO: What?

ALICE: "I can't, the highway is pink." "Then shoot me for godsake." "I can't, this is a dessert cheese."

BOO: What are we talking about?

ALICE *(Exiting)*: You could just say my breath smells, it's fine.

GRIEVER *(Quietly under Alice and Boo)*: And her husband Norbert. *(Begins putting on socks and shoes)* Norbert is embarrassed for all the little people . . . The little people are ashamed . . . And Stan Hopewell, the maker of so many pretty little shoes, is proud to be ashamed of queen Debbie, who by a strange coincidence of marriage and surgery is in fact her own uncle—by marriage to what should have been her second cousin once removed but is now as I say by a fluke of bloodmanship a small but elegant . . . electric peanut. *(Picks up brush to polish shoes, treats it as an Academy Award)* Thank you. Thank you. This means so much to me. I would never have been able to play this part if not for the unerring dedication, the unquestioned brilliance and the small shoes of . . . Yo mothuh! That's right I said yo muthuh! Yo!

ALICE *(Back on, munching a cracker)*: I'm going to get flowers.

BOO: Why are you eating? Where are you going?

GRIEVER *(Overlapping)*: Yo, Stella!

ALICE *(From off)*: I'M GOING TO GET FLOWERS, GRANDMOTHER!

GRIEVER *(Overlapping)*: STELLLLAAAAAAA! *(Exits, reenters on Motown music with hair dryer)*

ALICE *(Pops head in door)*: Relax, mia amore, bambina! *(Blows kisses and exits)*

GRIEVER *(Does Diana Ross in Central Park)*: Thank you. Thank you thank you thank you. And now go home. Go home and drive safely. *(Aims hair dryer at his face to create the storm)* Leave the park now. It's raining too hard. I know, I know, but the safest thing is for us all to leave, so I want you to move slowly and safely, directly out of the park. Be careful of your neighbor. I want you to turn to the man next to you and I want you to slit his throat. I want you to spill his blood, motherfucker . . . *(Hair dryer off; it becomes a microphone)* Thank you. There isn't anything I can say.

(Libby has returned with a drink; reading the back of the rum bottle, she has discovered a recipe and dials the phone.)

GRIEVER: I love you. I do. You're my main . . . main . . . mlaaaaa. Mlaaaa-mlaaaaaa. We're tired now, good night.

(He exits; phone rings.)

TOM: Which sounds better? *(Plays guitar)*

(Griever returns, answers phone.)

GRIEVER: I am out the door.
LIBBY: Just tell me if this sounds tacky. One part rum—one part undiluted pineapple juice concentrate—
GRIEVER *(Overlapping)*: It sounds tacky. Tacky, tacky . . .
LIBBY: —from a can, listen, one part triple sec, grenadine, lemon or—
TOM: Or. *(Plays another version)*
LIBBY: —lime slices and confectionary sugar to taste.
GRIEVER: Where does it say about the glucose tolerance test we're all going to have to take when we get to the hospital—?
LIBBY *(Hanging up before he has finished his sentence)*: Good-bye.
GRIEVER: Good-bye. Good-bye.

(Tom has stopped playing.)

TOM: None of the above?

LIBBY *(Making the punch)*: I really love your books, Alice. No. You know what I love, Alice? May I? Call you? By the way I am absolutely crazy about your books, oh sure, hasn't everybody? Bleah. Oh, are you a writer? I didn't realize that. Alice Fisher, my God. Everyone, this is Alice Fisher and her lover, Boo Boo.

GRIEVER *(Trying on shirts)*: No.

LIBBY: So how's the new book coming along, Alice? What? Are you serious? You can't stop writing. You're one of the best writers of our generation—

GRIEVER *(Holding up another shirt)*: No.

LIBBY: My generation—

GRIEVER: No.

LIBBY: Your generation. How old are you, Alice? Seriously, would you mind inscribing my copy of *Glissando*? Oh sure, I've only read it about ten times. My favorite character? Well, I'd have to say I liked them all equally . . . There's only one? Character. Well, it's just she's like so many different people I know . . . He. Is. Soooooo you *(Dialing)* girls are lesbians.

GRIEVER *(Shirt after shirt; under Libby)*: Charming, but—. No . . . Well, how you say—. No. Thank you . . . No. Very nice and . . . No. No thank you. No no no . . . No . . . Nnnnnnnnnnmaybe . . . No.

TOM: This is the bridge.

(Phone rings; Griever answers.)

GRIEVER: I've left, I'm on my way—

LIBBY *(Not waiting for him to finish)*: Stop on your way and pick up a copy of Alice Fisher's new book would you please for me?

GRIEVER: I want you to listen to the sound of my voice.

LIBBY: I can't.

GRIEVER: Take a deeeep breath.

LIBBY: I can't, I can't—

GRIEVER: Iiiiiiinnnnnnn—

LIBBY: I'm having a breakdown. *(Hangs up)* I love your books, I just read the new one, I mean, I just bought the new one, but—I lent it, what a great title, I loved it, I love your new book, what's it called? What I love, Alice, what I really really love about your books are the covers, I always judge a book by its cover, don't you? No, seriously, I love the way you weave all the different strands together, all the different people in different places doing different things, it's like modern music. How is it like modern music? . . . I don't know. *(She dials)*

GRIEVER *(Speaking under Libby; about shirts)*: YES! Yes, yes, yes! . . . No . . . Yes . . . No . . . Nnnnnnnnnnnnnnnn-yes . . . No . . . Maybe . . . Maybe . . . Maybe . . . Nnnnnooo . . . Maybe . . .

TOM *(Speaking under Libby)*: See, it takes a long time to resolve and then it just goes to the same refrain over and over, you know, like a Chinese screen. It's like one stroke and that's the whole thing. I wish I had . . . I can hear it . . . *(Singing and playing)* "I came here to— . . . I came down to . . ." . . . something . . . "I came here from—" . . . "They all want the same thing . . ."

(Boo exits to take a shower. Griever answers the phone; he and Libby speak over Tom's song.)

GRIEVER: I am in the taxi—

LIBBY: It's off.

GRIEVER: I am there, I'm ringing your bell—

LIBBY: No, I'm not going to be here, I'm going to the movies—

GRIEVER: Listen to me please—

LIBBY: I died.

GRIEVER: It is the guest's responsibility to have a good time. You provide the space—

LIBBY: I got sick and died.

GRIEVER: Then it is up to the guest.

TOM *(Calling offstage)*: What's the story?

GRIEVER: If he or she does not choose to have a good time—

LIBBY: They won't.

TOM *(Simultaneously with Libby)*: Are we going?

GRIEVER: There is nothing you can do about it.

TOM: Are we going?

GRIEVER: Conversely, no amount of burnt food, bad wine, cheap cocaine or hideous furnishings—

TOM: Em?

GRIEVER: —can prevent the truly convivial spirit from having a pleasant evening in the company of his or her peers.

LIBBY: Thank you.

GRIEVER: Now go vomit. I will be right—

(She hangs up.)

—there, good-bye—

TOM: Baby?

GRIEVER: —good-bye, good-bye— *(The right shirt)* Yes! . . . yes, yes, yes!

LIBBY *(Overlapping)*: No, I love your books, I really do. I said I love your books, Alice, don't you know how to take a compliment? That's not a very attractive trait, Alice. Maybe that's something you'd like to think about, work on with your friend, your lesbian, lover, doctor friend, I'll tell you something, Alice.

(Alice enters.)

You lay down with psychiatrists, you get up with flaws.

ALICE: It's warm.

LIBBY *(On her exit)*: No, I love your books, really, *Catcher in the Raw*, for instance.

BOO *(From off)*: Time to go?

ALICE: If only I hadn't run into her in the elevator that day.

(Boo enters, drying her hair with a towel.)

I was just so pleased I remembered her name. I hate that name, it sounds like something you put on Indian food: Libby. Please pass the Libby.

BOO: Are we going as we are or, uh—?

ALICE: It's all my fault. Why don't I call and say I'm sick, I don't mind . . . You hate me.

(Boo exits as Emily enters from the outside.)

TOM: What was that all about?

EMILY: You were working.

TOM: I'm having a conversation with myself like an asshole.

EMILY: Oh. I'm sorry.

TOM: . . . Nice out?

EMILY: Yeah. How'd it go?

TOM: Good. Needs words.

EMILY: Can I hear?

TOM: Well, are we going?

EMILY: Oh—I'll just fix my hair.

(She exits as Boo comes back on, wearing a different blouse.)

EMILY: Who are these people, remind me.

LIBBY *(Reenters in black cocktail dress)*: Alice, Boo, Emily, Tom . . .

TOM: Nobody. Listen, this part is pretty.

ALICE: We can stay in . . . How 'bout if we have a signal for when one of us wants to leave?

BOO: I'll just scream.

ALICE: Or I could say something like . . .

BOO: Time to go now.

ALICE: That's good.

(Boo goes off.)

LIBBY *(Under Alice and Boo; introduces the place cards to one another)*: Alice, this is Tom. Tom, this is Alice. Alice,

Emily, Booby, Boober . . . BooBoo . . . Bee Boo
Boo . . . Booby Boo Boo . . . Bebe Rebozo . . . Bobby
Goldsboro . . . *(Throws place cards away)*

TOM: Do you want to hear this?

GRIEVER *(Trying on the first tie)*: Nope.

EMILY *(From off)*: I'm listening. *(Enters)* Sorry.

ALICE *(Calling to offstage)*: You look terrific!

GRIEVER: No way.

TOM: Okay. It has like a melody—sort of a descant over the
top.

(Boo reenters, tying a sash around her waist.)

EMILY: Uh-huh.

ALICE: I, on the other hand, look like an old, used . . .

TOM: And the whole thing should be on a piano, but we
don't have a piano, so . . .

(Norbert exits.)

BOO: True. Let's go.

TOM: All right?

ALICE: It's right downstairs.

TOM: It needs words.

BOO: Then let's be early.

EMILY: Okay.

BOO: Nouvelle chic.

(Libby goes out again; Tom plays.)

ALICE: You just want to see her with her hair wet.

BOO: Absolutely.

ALICE *(Looking in compact mirror)*: Wait. God.

BOO: You look fine.

ALICE: I don't want anybody to think I labored to look this . . .

EMILY: Pretty.

ALICE: Unlabored.

EMILY: I like it.

ALICE: It's true:

TOM: Wait, this is the melody.

GRIEVER: Tooooooooo.

TOM: I mean, it's not in the accompaniment . . . Well, you'll see . . . I know what it should say, too, but . . . Like this . . .

ALICE *(Simultaneously with Tom)*: You have to put yourself together a little bit or people think you think you're so cool you don't have to put yourself together.

BOO *(Exiting yet again)*: Vanity, vanity, all is . . .

TOM: Without words. *(Plays)*

ALICE: I'm so vain I prob'ly think this song is about me.

(Libby reenters with hors d'oeuvres; she tries to get top off caviar jar.)

TOM: Or something. It keeps repeating.

BOO *(From off)*: Fairfield Porter?

ALICE: The—? Famous?

BOO *(Entering)*: Painter?

ALICE: Right.

BOO: When asked if he thought it was vain to sign one's paintings or not to sign one's paintings . . .

ALICE: Right.

BOO: Said—

ALICE: To sign or not to sign.

BOO: Right.

TOM: This is the bridge.

ALICE: Said?

BOO: If you're vain, it's vain to sign your paintings and it's vain not to sign your paintings.

ALICE: Ah-ha.

(Libby bangs caviar jar twice on tabletop.)

BOO: And if you're not vain, then it's not vain to sign your paintings and it's not vain—

ALICE AND BOO: Not to sign your paintings.

ALICE: Too true. And we would say that I am—?
EMILY: It's like a folk song.

> *(Trying to open the caviar jar with her teeth, Libby breaks her cap.)*

LIBBY: Ow!

> *(Tom stops playing.)*

EMILY: It's not like a folk song.

> *(Libby spits out her tooth.)*

ALICE: No comment. All right, let's go.
TOM *(Overlapping)*: Let's go.
EMILY: It isn't.
TOM: It is, come on.

> *(Alice is headed for the door; Norbert returns in different clothes, picks up puzzle and orange peel, exits.)*

BOO: Flowers.
EMILY: It's pretty.
TOM: Yeah.
EMILY: I like it.
ALICE: This is why I keep you around.
TOM: It's supposed to be the way it is, exactly the way it is.

> *(Emily and Tom continue under Alice and Boo.)*

ALICE: All right, what's our signal?
BOO: You say, Did anybody see that article in the *Times* on DNA? And I'll say—
ALICE: No, I didn't see that—
BOO: Wasn't it incredible?
ALICE: Oh, okay, wasn't it—

BOO: No, if I want to leave I'll say yes and if I don't I'll say no.

ALICE: Good.

EMILY: I know.

TOM: The words are . . . completely unsentimental—

EMILY: Uh-huh.

TOM: They're flat, like I did this and I did this and I—

(Libby has dialed; phone rings. Griever answers; speaks under Tom, Alice and Boo.)

GRIEVER: Walk directly to your front door and by the time you get there I will be there. *(Hangs up)*

LIBBY: Grieve?

EMILY: I like it.

ALICE: Wait.

BOO: What?

ALICE: I love you.

TOM: I like you.

GRIEVER *(One last look in the mirror)*: Yes!

(Blackout. Lights up to half. The actors move the sculptural pieces into their positions for the party. Tom's ottoman becomes the coffee table; Griever's dressing table becomes a chair, etc. In the half-light we see Alice present Libby with the flowers; she places them in a vase. All of this is under-scored with melancholy piano music. As the party lights come up all the actors are frozen in position: Boo and Griever at the punch bowl, Norbert down left, Tom and Emily on the sofa, Alice upstage center and Libby standing by the vase. Large pillows have been placed on the floor around the coffee table. As Alice speaks the characters are released from their freeze.)

SCENE 2

ALICE: There's this whole theory, all right?

(Griever fills Boo's punch glass.)

BOO: Here we go.

ALICE: That the experiential part of the brain—the right? Hemisphere?

BOO *(Overlapping)*: Don't look at me.

ALICE: And the side responsible for assigning the words . . .

GRIEVER: Right.

ALICE: No, the left. Ha ha. Are incompatible.

GRIEVER: Alice.

ALICE: Essentially. Essentially.

BOO: Wellllll—

ALICE: They don't communicate.

BOO: If they didn't communicate—

ALICE: They barely communicate, I'm telling this, if you want to make up your own theory—

BOO: That's right—

ALICE: When I'm finished making up mine . . .

GRIEVER: The experiential part and the part—

ALICE: Right. And there's just this little thread connecting the two. Called—the corpus cassolum.

GRIEVER: I knew that.

ALICE: Right?

BOO: Callosum.

ALICE: Callosum, the corpus callosum. And that's all there is.

(Libby exits into the kitchen.)

So everything that happens in the right side of the brain and everything that happens in the left side of the brain has to pass through this little thread. If the right hand is to know what the left hand is doing so to speak.

GRIEVER: Write that down.

ALICE: Anyway. You're trying to capture the intangible.

GRIEVER: Uh-huh?

(Libby reenters with a tray of canapés which she takes from guest to guest.)

ALICE: And you can't. Because the experience doesn't want to be captured. The way primitive peoples don't want to have their pictures taken.

BOO: Why are you looking at me?

ALICE: So you're constantly jumping back and forth: "What did that feel like?" "What do you call that?" And the words are always less. Or maybe I'm just a mediocre writer.

BOO: Right.

ALICE: So the thing that—

LIBBY *(Serving Alice, simultaneously)*: Oh, I really love—

ALICE: I'm sorry.

LIBBY *(Holding her top lip in place with one finger)*: I say I really love your writing.

ALICE: Oh, thank you. Thank you. No, it's, you know, that feeling of its being right on the tip of your tongue.

GRIEVER: Right.

TOM *(Simultaneously)*: Uh-huh.

ALICE: And nine hundred and ninety-nine times out of a thousand: smoke, nothing, blah.

GRIEVER: I hate that. Don't you? When you can't . . . when you can't . . . think of something. *(Laughs; to Libby)* Smile.

(She does, without showing teeth.)

That's better.

ALICE: So you can't wait for inspiration is my point.

GRIEVER: Uh-huh.

ALICE: That's all. You have to work.

GRIEVER: Right.

ALICE: Which is why I'm such a bore to live with.

(Libby is serving Boo.)

BOO: Here, here, I'll drink to that.

GRIEVER: But . . .

BOO: This punch is so tacky, I love it.

LIBBY *(Toward the wall)*: Thanks.

GRIEVER: All right. How do you know . . . ? You'll have to forgive me, I'm illiterate. But . . . I mean, how do you know—? Or—I mean . . . Come on, Griever, you can do it.

ALICE: See, you could never name a character Griever, for instance, without everybody wanting to know what's he grieving?

GRIEVER: Right.

ALICE: For. Is it grieving for or grieving?

BOO: Grieving for.

LIBBY *(Simultaneously with Boo)*: Grieving.

ALICE: Is it?

TOM: Grieving for, I think.

ALICE: I never learned any grammar either, so—anyway, how do you know what?

GRIEVER: Well, how do you know—? I mean, do you know everything that's going to happen in a certain story?

ALICE: No.

GRIEVER: Before you start?

ALICE: I don't. You just—jump off the cliff. You're bound to land somewhere. And you never know—I mean—if I might borrow an expression of yours, madame—

BOO: Please.

ALICE: —you don't know what's going to be poop on ice, you don't know what's going to be a masterpiece.

BOO *(Overlapping)*: What?

GRIEVER: What is it, poop on ice?

BOO: I do not say that. She made that up, I swear. Tell them I do not say poop on ice, please.

ALICE *(Simultaneously; under Boo and Griever)*: You have to hear it first and see—hear how it sounds. I thought my last book was going to be one of the great tomes of Western literature; it turned out to be, what? Something like eighty-two pages . . .

GRIEVER: Poop? On ice?

BOO: I've never even met her, I swear to God.

TOM: I'm listening.

ALICE: Anyway, enough about me, what did *you* think of my last book?

(Alice smiles at her own joke. Norbert crosses to the bar, takes a second beer.)

BOO: I do not say poop on ice.

ALICE: No, she doesn't, I was just making that up. *(Mouths)* She does.

(Boo sits on the floor with her back to the audience.)

LIBBY: You know what scene in one of your books I love?

ALICE: No.

LIBBY: I love the scene where they're all sitting around—

GRIEVER: Take your hand away from your mouth.

LIBBY: Oh.

GRIEVER: We can't hear you.

LIBBY: It itches. Well, I love all your books, I really do.

GRIEVER: No, you were going to say which scene.

ALICE: Yes!

LIBBY: No, I don't know, I love all those scenes, I can't think of which one I meant, I can't.

ALICE: I was just getting excited.

LIBBY: I love them all, I really do.

ALICE: Well, you have good taste.

TOM: I haven't read any of your books, I'm sorry.

(Libby is going toward kitchen; Griever catches her arm.)

ALICE: Oh, please, I'm always so surprised when one copy of one book sells. *(To Boo)* And don't you say one word.

GRIEVER *(Simultaneously; mouthed, to Libby)*: You all right? . . . You sure?

(Libby exits.)

BOO: But you know what I always notice?

ALICE: What? What do you notice? Can I have a sip of your punch?

BOO: People don't relate to the words at all. It's as if—in anything, plays, books, movies—it's as if there was something behind the words.

ALICE: Intention.

GRIEVER *(Simultaneously)*: Uh-huh?

BOO: Either behind the words or beyond the words—

ALICE: Intention.

BOO: May I say this?

ALICE: Sorry.

BOO: You got to make up your theory.

ALICE: You're absolutely right.

BOO: I mean . . . Eugene O'Neill, all right?

ALICE: Ugh.

BOO: But that's my point. There's something besides the words—beyond the words.

(Norbert sits.)

ALICE: Yes, but there's also—

BOO: Wait. Okay, O'Neill in one sense could not write.

TOM: *Eugene* O'Neill?

(Libby returns. Griever talks to her under Boo and Tom.)

BOO: In one sense. Really, go see them again, they're—his plays—

TOM: Uh-huh.

BOO: Very clunky and self-indulgent.

TOM: *Long Day's Journey into Night?*

GRIEVER: The flowers look beautiful, don't they?

LIBBY: Mm-hm.

GRIEVER: The place looks great.

BOO *(Simultaneously with Griever)*: But they're not just about the words, that's what I'm trying to say. It's true, they appear to have been written by a seventh grader if you're just listening. But—

TOM *(Overlapping)*: Didn't he win a Nobel Prize or something?

BOO: Yes, but—obviously something transcends—

ALICE *(Simultaneously with Boo)*: Oh please, Knut Hamsun won the Nobel Prize, Hermann Hesse!

TOM: I love Hermann Hesse.

ALICE: *Steppenwolf?*

TOM: I love *Steppenwolf.*

ALICE: Well, as a teenager I did too, but have you gone back? I mean—

BOO: There's nothing wrong with that. I thought Thomas Wolfe was the greatest writer who ever lived. Everything doesn't have to be for adults.

GRIEVER: I don't read and I'm proud of it.

BOO: A. E. Housman.

ALICE: Beatrix Potter.

BOO: Oh, Gore Vidal? Has . . . says that since we don't read anymore?

ALICE: When did we?

TOM: Uh-huh?

ALICE *(To Griever)*: No offense.

BOO: Well, he says that too, but since we don't read anymore, since we get most of our information from television and movies—from images—

EMILY: Uh-huh?

BOO: That we lose the ability to think. Literally. Linearly. That's hard to say.

GRIEVER: Linearly.

BOO: That, in other words, across the page from left to right or top to bottom if you're Japanese or whatever it is—

GRIEVER: Mmmmmmmm.

BOO: That thought is sequential. The logic is . . .

ALICE: Linear.

BOO: And if we grow up with movies and TV and we lose the entire . . . Well, anyway, I think he's wrong, I do.

GRIEVER: Gore Vidal? Wrong?

BOO: I think—yes.

GRIEVER: I'm going to tell him you said that.

BOO *(Crossing to bowl of mixed nuts)*: I think philosophy and ideas—I think film and television are perfectly capable of conveying thought. I know you don't.

ALICE: You don't think that.

BOO: Why not?

GRIEVER: Can I get anybody anything—more punch there, Boo?

BOO: Yes, please, thanks. I love this.

GRIEVER: Lib? Norb? You okay? Anybody?

ALICE *(Overlapping)*: A word stands for something.

BOO: So does a picture.

ALICE: I don't see how you can say that a succession of images—

BOO: People talk in movies—

ALICE: Come on—

BOO: And they're sequential too, they're linear, you just can't go back and reread.

ALICE: What does *La Dolce Vita* mean? What are the ideas? Your guess is as good as mine.

BOO: Oh, we're going to be in Italy in three weeks and I've never been, I'm so excited.

GRIEVER *(Overlapping)*: Libby was just there.

BOO: Really? Is it beautiful?

LIBBY: Oh . . . *(Turning her face front)* Very.

BOO: Oh, I want to hear all about it. All right, I'm sorry, what does *La Dolce Vita* mean? Who knows, who cares?

ALICE: That's my point exactly—

BOO *(Overlapping)*: What does *The Penal Colony* mean, what does *Moby Dick* mean?

ALICE: You can't—you're talking about fiction and you're talking about thought, you can't. All fiction is open to interpretation.

BOO: So is philosophy.

GRIEVER *(With drinks)*: She's got you there, Al.

BOO: Thanks.

ALICE: You can't make a movie out of Descartes.

BOO: Why not?

ALICE: His ideas?

BOO: Why not?

ALICE: Because. You can't.

BOO: Why not?

ALICE: Ideas do not come across in pictures, all right?

BOO: Why not?

GRIEVER: I think you're going to have to come up with another argument.

ALICE *(Overlapping)*: Ideas are not—words are ideas.

BOO: Pictures are ideas.

ALICE: They're not, they're pictures. They don't stand for anything, they are the thing.

BOO: No, they're not, the thing is three-dimensional.

ALICE: You know what I'm saying, come on—

BOO: I think you're wrong. Buster Keaton falling off of a . . . what?

GRIEVER: Train.

BOO: Thank you.

GRIEVER: I love making a contribution.

LIBBY *(Mouthed)*: Excuse me.

GRIEVER *(To Libby)*: Do you want some help?

LIBBY *(As she exits)*: Nope.

GRIEVER: You sure?

LIBBY *(From off)*: Yep, stay there.

BOO *(Continuing over Griever and Libby)*: Is a symbol. If you read that someone in a little porkpie hat falls off a train, why is that any more representative or less open

to interpretation than the actual image of Buster
Keaton falling off—it's more—open to interpretation
than the visual, because you can't fill in the details,
they're there.

ALICE: I understand—

BOO: When I read the word *train* I can have a thousand different trains, but Buster Keaton's train is one very spe-
cific train—

ALICE: But there's not the idea of train, that's my point;
there's train and then there's Buster Keaton's train.

GRIEVER *(Sits on the floor)*: Wait, I'm lost.

ALICE: Well, that's because you don't read.

GRIEVER: Right.

ALICE *(Jovial)*: Anyway. *(She crosses to the bar, then sits by it)*

GRIEVER *(Lighting a cigarette)*: What do you do, Emily?

EMILY: I'm a secretary.

GRIEVER: Oh really? Where?

EMILY: Just a company.

GRIEVER: Uh-huh.

EMILY: Midtown.

ALICE: What's it called?

GRIEVER *(Simultaneously)*: What's it called? *(To Alice)* You
owe me a coke.

ALICE: All right.

EMILY: Um . . . I feel like I'm on the Merv Griffin show.

GRIEVER: Relax, honey, we're all pulling for you, everybody
loves you.

EMILY: It's called Scientific Abstracts and I really hate talking about it on my day off.

GRIEVER: Okay.

BOO: Oh, here's to that, God almighty I hate thinking about
work on Sunday. Let's talk about . . . I don't know.
What shall we talk about?

TOM: What kind of work do you do? Oh, you just said . . .

BOO: That's right. I'm a family therapist.

TOM: Oh.

BOO *(She cracks up)*: I do family therapy . . . So.

EMILY: What's family therapy?

(Boo laughs again.)

EMILY: Oh, you just said—

BOO: No, that's all right, that's all right. Family therapy. All right, you have a problem.

NORBERT: Okay.

BOO: You come to me. I would probably say, "This guy is past help." No, I'm tired, I'm sorry. Family therapy . . . Why can't I think of this?

ALICE: How much punch have you had?

BOO: I know this, I know this, this is what I do.

GRIEVER: Sure it is.

BOO: Family therapy. All right: say you're a drug addict.

NORBERT: I'm a drug addict.

BOO: That's funny, you don't look like a drug addict. No, really, really, I really do do this, doo-doo. I am bomb-o.

ALICE: I would say.

BOO: No, instead of treating you—instead of treating the problem as if you carry full responsibility—

NORBERT: Uh-huh.

BOO: And spending five years on the couch trying to analyze and understand all your wishes and your fears—

NORBERT: Right.

BOO: Which is fine. But expensive and long and painful and not always successful.

GRIEVER: But other than that, Mrs. Lincoln.

BOO: Really. We try to look at the dynamics of the family and see if . . . we can't blame somebody else for it. No, I'm sorry. Usually in a family structure there's one person who acts out—they drink or they flunk out in school—

NORBERT: Right.

BOO: Or they steal cars. But in my experience they are not necessarily the problem.

NORBERT: They're the symptom.

BOO: Yes. So that often a child who supposedly has learning difficulties—

NORBERT: Uh-huh.

BOO: Is really refusing to learn to read, say, because he knows damn well his father'll beat the shit out of him if he does.

GRIEVER: What? Learn to read.

BOO *(Simultaneously)*: Learn to read.

GRIEVER: Right.

BOO: The father can't read.

GRIEVER: I gotcha.

BOO: So that's what I do.

GRIEVER: Beat the shit out of 'em?

BOO: But I want to hear more about skydiving. I can't believe we're talking about family therapy. What's it like? Where do you do it? What's it cost? Where did you learn to do it? Why do you do it?

GRIEVER: In that order.

NORBERT: All right. Um, it's fun—that's why I do it. And Red Bank, New Jersey is where and I learned in the army.

BOO: Oh.

NORBERT: And what else?

GRIEVER: How much does it cost?

NORBERT: Right. It costs about eighty dollars for your first day.

BOO: Oh, that's cheap.

NORBERT: That includes five hours on the ground learning how to fall, how to land, how to fold your parachute, pull your ripcord.

ALICE: You don't actually jump out of the plane on your first day.

NORBERT: Sure.

ALICE: God. But you don't skydive on your first day.

NORBERT: Sure you do.

ALICE: But not free-fall, I mean.

NORBERT: Sure you do.

BOO: Does Libby do that?

NORBERT *(Going for a cracker)*: Well, we're having a little trouble getting Libby out of the plane. But—first we take you up on what's called a static line—you have a simulated ripcord, your chute opens automatically, then—

TOM: How high are you?

NORBERT: Right now?

TOM: Right.

BOO *(Simultaneously)*: Really.

NORBERT: No, we start you at three thousand feet, that's the minimum and then—

BOO *(Overlapping)*: Three thousand feet.

NORBERT: Right—and then we go up three hundred feet, increments of three hundred feet per jump; seventy-five hundred feet is about tops for a student jump.

BOO: How fast do you fall?

NORBERT: You start at sixty feet per second—

BOO: Start.

NORBERT: And you always open your chute at three thousand feet, so from seventy-five hundred feet you have a twenty-six second free fall; from twelve thousand feet which is your ceiling you have a seventy second free fall.

BOO: Jesus Christ.

EMILY: How many people forget to pull their ripcords?

NORBERT: Some, actually—

BOO *(Overlapping)*: They do?

NORBERT: Well, sure. It's against your body's instincts to jump. I mean, you look out that blue window and you see the ground all the way down there and your gut says, no way, sometimes—

GRIEVER: What do you do if they don't jump?

NORBERT: Push 'em. No, we go back and repeat the instructions. If after three or four days it looks like it's not going to happen, we refund your money.

BOO: That's nice.

ALICE: Food smells good, doesn't it? *(She crosses to the coffee table, sits on the floor)*

NORBERT *(Simultaneously with Alice)*: You should all come out and try it. I'll give you a complimentary lesson.

(Libby reenters.)

BOO: Now there's an offer.

GRIEVER: Food smells great, kiddo.

ALICE *(Simultaneously under Griever)*: We're just hearing about your adventures. Norbert says you haven't quite gotten—

GRIEVER: Tell 'em about Italy, come on. *(To Alice)* Sorry.

BOO *(Overlapping)*: Oh, that's right, I want to hear about Italy, I want to hear about Italy. Is it gorgeous?

LIBBY: Oh, absolutely.

BOO: Oh, God.

ALICE: Where did you stay?

LIBBY: You mean hotels?

ALICE: No, I mean what cities.

LIBBY: Oh . . .

GRIEVER: Venice.

LIBBY: Venice. And . . . I can't think.

ALICE: Well. Anywhere in Italy.

LIBBY: Siena.

ALICE: Oh God, Siena.

LIBBY: Mmmmmm.

ALICE: The light?

LIBBY: Wonderful.

GRIEVER: What is the matter with your mouth?

LIBBY: It itches, Griever.

GRIEVER: Sorry.

BOO: Well, I can't wait, I really can't. So far I can say . . . what?

ALICE: We've been on a crash course for the last three weeks.

BOO: Crash is right. Um—la mama . . . una mama—

ALICE: La mia mama—

BOO: La mia mama . . .

GRIEVER *(Overlapping)*: Mama mia, that's a spicy speecy— remember that? . . . No?

ALICE *(Overlapping)*: All'—

BOO: All'aeroporto.

ALICE: Brava.

BOO: La mia mama e all'aeroporto. My mother is at the airport.

GRIEVER: That should come in handy.

BOO: What else?

ALICE: Facciamo—

BOO: Facciamo—

ALICE: Un giro.

BOO *(Drops to her knees onto one of the pillows)*: Facciamo un giro . . . Facciamo un giro . . .

GRIEVER: They'll starve to death before she can order a meal, but—no problem.

BOO *(Overlapping)*: Facciamo—shut up! Facciamo un giro . . .

ALICE: In—

BOO: In macchina all'aeroporto.

ALICE: Vorrebbe guidare?

BOO: Si.

ALICE: No, come on.

BOO: Um . . .

TOM: Do you mind if I put on some music?

LIBBY: No.

TOM: I know where it is.

(He goes into the next room; Emily follows him out.)

BOO: Vorrebbe . . . Vorrebbe . . .

GRIEVER *(Overlapping; sings to the tune of "Volare")*: Vorrebbe! Whoa-ho-ho-ho!

BOO: Christ—mi . . . Mi . . .

ALICE: Piacerebbe.

BOO: Mi piacerebbe molto. Alice speaks about seven languages fluently.

ALICE: That's not even remotely true but . . .

GRIEVER *(Simultaneously with Alice)*: Not me. I can barely speak English . . . Never travel . . .

BOO: I love what you've done with your apartment, Libby.

LIBBY: Thanks.

BOO: Do you entertain a lot?

LIBBY *(Lighting her and Boo's cigarettes)*: No. Actually, this is the first time since I moved in.

BOO: Haven't you lived here . . . ?

(Angular jazz piano music.)

LIBBY: Four years.

BOO: Oh.

(Tom and Emily return to their positions on the sofa.)

ALICE: What's this?

TOM: Cecil Taylor?

ALICE: Oh.

BOO: Who's that?

ALICE: Cecil Taylor? You've never heard of him?

BOO: Can I still stay at the party? Who's Cecil Taylor?

GRIEVER: He's very famous, Boo.

BOO: I gathered.

GRIEVER: I never heard of him either.

TOM: He's like the most technically proficient jazz pianist in the world.

BOO: Really?

TOM: Yeah, he literally alters the landscape of what you can do musically.

BOO: Really?

TOM: Yeah, he's real good.

BOO: Are you a musician?

TOM: Mm-hm.

LIBBY: Tom's a wonderful composer.

TOM: Oh, yeah, right—

LIBBY: You are.

TOM: No, I'm a studio musician. I do a lot of studio work.

BOO: Are you saying Libby lied to us, Tom?

LIBBY *(Mouthed)*: He's wonderful.

TOM: But I don't know if you can hear it, but I mean, he's literally rethinking what you can do with melody. He's changing all the rules from the ground up. He's taking all your expectations and kind of . . .

GRIEVER: I don't understand what you mean *melody.*

(Libby gets up and heads for the kitchen.)

TOM: Throwing them back at you.

GRIEVER *(Simultaneously with Tom, to Libby)*: You want some help? *(To Tom)* Sorry.

LIBBY *(From off)*: Nope.

GRIEVER: Are you sure?

LIBBY: Yep.

GRIEVER *(To Tom)*: I'm sorry.

TOM: Like a painter. He's breaking it up, you know, and putting some parts of it in front of where they belong and he's splitting up tonalities and colors, shapes—

ALICE: Splitting up did you say?

TOM: Splitting.

ALICE: No, I know, I was . . .

TOM: He's literally challenging you to hear it, you know, rehear it. What is music?

GRIEVER: No, I know, but this isn't like a famous melody? Or—?

TOM: Why not?

GRIEVER: I mean it isn't like "Raindrops on roses and whiskers on kittens" backwards or something.

TOM: No . . .

GRIEVER: No, I know what you're saying.

(Pause. They all listen.)

I know what you're saying. *(Pause)* But . . . *(Pause)* Does anybody else get depressed on Sunday nights?

BOO: Always.

GRIEVER: I do.

BOO: I always get depressed.

GRIEVER: I could be having the best time, I don't know what it is.

ALICE: You don't always get depressed.

BOO: That's what I was feeling upstairs.

ALICE: Still, you don't always get—

BOO: You know what it is? It's having to go to school in the morning.

GRIEVER: Is that it?

BOO: I think so.

ALICE *(Overlapping)*: She doesn't always get depressed.

BOO: All right, I don't always get depressed.

GRIEVER: I think it's Ed Sullivan.

BOO: Now that's interesting.

GRIEVER: I think—no, you know what I think it is? I know what it is!

BOO: What?

GRIEVER: I think it's Topo Gigio.

BOO: Who?

GRIEVER: I really think it was Topo Gigio.

ALICE: I remember Topo Gigio.

GRIEVER: Right?

ALICE: I loved Topo Gigio.

GRIEVER: Really?

ALICE: Yes, don't you remember?

GRIEVER: You loved Topo Gigio?

BOO: Who's Topo Gigio?

ALICE: Topo Gigio was this little mouse, Italian mouse—

BOO: Oh yes.

ALICE: Remember?

BOO: Right, right.

ALICE: Topo Gigio, I loved Topo Gigio.

BOO: You loved Top Gigio?

ALICE: Yes. Is that like Lawrence Welk or something? I thought he was cute.

BOO: He was.

GRIEVER: He was cute.

ALICE: I want to die all of a sudden. I don't know what it is. I loved—yes, I loved Topo Gigio, take me away.

GRIEVER: Anyway—

ALICE *(To Emily)*: Do you remember Topo Gigio?

EMILY: Mm-hm.
ALICE: You do. Did you like him?

(Emily shakes her head no.)

God.
GRIEVER: Anyway, you know, he was always going: "Eddie! I love you Eddie! Kiss me!"
BOO: That's very good.
ALICE *(To Tom)*: Did you hate him too?

(He did.)

GRIEVER: Right? I just remember he was the last thing on the show and he came on . . .
ALICE *(Simultaneously; under Griever)*: Everybody. No wonder you get depressed on Sundays.
BOO: Shhhh!
ALICE: I will too from now on. Forever and ever. *(Crosses to bar unit)*
GRIEVER *(Overlapping Alice)*: Maybe you're right, maybe it's because I knew I had to go to bed.
BOO *(To Griever)*: Uh-huh?
GRIEVER: But I just remember this tremendous feeling of sadness. Emptiness. I think that's why I never wanted to go to Italy.
ALICE: Because of Topo Gigio? Oh come on.

(Norbert and Alice continue under Boo and Griever.)

BOO *(To Tom)*: Can we turn this down? I like it, it's just . . . It's not really party music.

(Tom exits.)

(Calls from doorway) Don't turn it all the way off.
GRIEVER: Can I get anybody anything? Boober?
BOO: No thanks.

GRIEVER: Tom? . . . Anybody?

NORBERT *(To Alice)*: I liked him.

ALICE: You did? Would you say that again? Wait. *(She crosses up to the sofa unit, sits)* Excuse me, Dr. Weinstein . . . Doctor?

BOO: What?

ALICE: He liked Topo Gigio.

BOO: Well sure he did, he was probably two years old.

ALICE: Don't pay any attention to her. She's trying to take Topo Gigio away from us. Topo Gigio is immortal.

(During Alice and Boo's exchange, Griever moves to the doorway of the kitchen and stands there; Libby stands, arms folded. Lights dim on the party sequence as Tom returns to his permanent position on the sofa. Emily has separated from the group, faces the audience. Throughout the following conversation we see the party silhouetted, soundlessly enacted.)

GRIEVER: Congratulations, it's going great, don't you think? Everybody's having a good time, no fights. What's the matter? Am I being a jerk? My hair look stupid? What? Just tell me. I fucked up.

(Libby smiles broadly: no tooth.)

LIBBY: What do you think? Nice? I was going to do all of them, but I wanted to see how one looked first. I don't know, I can't decide.

GRIEVER: What did you do?

LIBBY: Do you think I'll be more successful on dates or what?

GRIEVER: What did you do?

LIBBY: I thought I was doing an incredible job, subtly hiding the fact that I look like Margaret Hamilton, and every two seconds you keep asking me what is the matter with my mouth.

GRIEVER: Well, honey pie—

LIBBY *(Not stopping)*: Because someone who was supposed to come early and help with the food didn't so I had to do everything by myself which is why I look like Margaret Hamilton.

GRIEVER: Dueling guilt trips—

LIBBY: And now the only thing that would make me happy would be for you to go back out there and be charming until everyone goes home and we can—

GRIEVER: Baby—

LIBBY: —begin to forget this whole hideous experience and someday maybe someday—

GRIEVER: Sugar butt—

LIBBY: —we might be able to pick up the shattered remains of our friendship and see what we might be able to—

GRIEVER: Liver lips—

LIBBY: —piece together over a drink if I'm in a good mood.

GRIEVER: First of all, Margaret Hamilton had all her teeth.

LIBBY: I'm so happy this amuses you.

GRIEVER: Second of all, you look fine, nobody notices, nobody would care, and it's cute. Let me see it again.

LIBBY: Why are you allowed to live?

GRIEVER: Let me see. Please?

LIBBY: If you say one word to anybody—

GRIEVER: Say cheese! Now how did we do this?

LIBBY: I was taking the lid off a caviar jar.

GRIEVER: And this is a cap, not a tooth.

LIBBY: This was a cap.

GRIEVER: This was a cap. So this does not hurt physically.

LIBBY: Spiritually.

GRIEVER: Now. You are not going to spend the rest of the evening grunting every time someone asks you a question.

LIBBY: I can if I want to.

GRIEVER: That's right, it's your party—

LIBBY: And I'll cry if I want to, it isn't funny.

GRIEVER: Maybe a little bit.

LIBBY: The whole thing was a horrible idea, I don't know anybody anymore, I didn't know who to invite . . .

GRIEVER: Everyone is having a great time—

LIBBY: I wasn't ready, Griever, I was not ready to do this.

GRIEVER: Yes you were.

LIBBY: Everybody knows.

GRIEVER *(Overlapping)*: They don't know. Now look at me . . . Stop . . .

LIBBY *(Overlapping)*: It's the wrong chemistry, nobody likes anybody, the food isn't ready and I look like a witch.

GRIEVER: Nobody knows anything, what if they did?

LIBBY: I'm not talking about the tooth.

GRIEVER: What if everybody knew everything? Well? What if they did? Tom knows. I know. We love you.

LIBBY: I can't—

(He tries to embrace her.)

Don't hold me. I'm sorry.

GRIEVER: It's all right.

LIBBY: Go say I'm having trouble with the sauce, don't let anybody in here.

GRIEVER: We can talk about this whole thing in group, all right?

LIBBY: I'm fine.

GRIEVER: You can tell everybody how horrible I was at your party.

LIBBY: Fine.

GRIEVER: I'm real proud of you, you know that. And you can't even notice it, all right, I lied.

LIBBY: Go!

GRIEVER: And I love you, don't forget that.

LIBBY: I'd rather have a big bag of money.

(Crossfade from kitchen to living room; lights and sound slowly up on the party scene as Libby disappears. Norbert and Tom are smoking a joint.)

NORBERT *(Simultaneously with Griever)*: The army is very weird, though. I mean, it's not like the real world.

TOM: Right.

NORBERT: You pretty much have to put your disbelief in suspension or whatever the—

ALICE *(Simultaneously with Norbert)*: I'm tired, aren't you?

BOO: No, I just want to eat something before I turn into a pineapple.

GRIEVER: What happened to Cecil Beaton?

ALICE: We bullied him into turning it off.

GRIEVER *(To Norbert)*: You're taking drugs, aren't you? I leave you alone for two seconds, give me that. *(Snatches joint, takes a long drag)*

BOO: Can we do anything to help?

GRIEVER: I wouldn't suggest going in there if I were you.

ALICE: Why?

BOO *(Simultaneously)*: Why?

ALICE: You owe me a coke!

GRIEVER: Then you owe it to me.

ALICE: Right.

GRIEVER: Libby, or Elizabeth as she is known to almost no one, is probably the world's most phenomenal control freak when it comes to cooking.

BOO: Ah.

GRIEVER *(To Norbert)*: Do you want this back? Can't have it. All right.

NORBERT: Ha-ha-ha.

GRIEVER: No, seriously, she'll break your legs if you go in there.

BOO: Oh I like a girl like that, don't you?

ALICE: Mmmm.

(Norbert hands joint to Emily. Piano music has appeared underneath this scene. It's the same melody that Tom has been working on.)

NORBERT: Emily.

GRIEVER: All right, I have a question for ze doctor.

EMILY: Thanks.

BOO: Hm?

GRIEVER: All right . . .

(Emily hands joint to Alice.)

ALICE: Thanks.

(A pin spot has slowly come up on Emily's face. All the other characters freeze and Emily sings to the piano accompaniment.)

EMILY:
        They all want the same thing.
        My mother'd been through it.
        She told me to remember
        They all want the same thing.
        My father left her.
        She had to raise me by herself.
        After going out a few times
        She gave up on replacements.
        Look around you.
        Look at your sister.
        Where did she find that guy?
        Someday soon he'll leave her.
        Just like your father.
        He went to California.
        He didn't even leave me
        For some other woman.

(The other characters unfreeze momentarily; Emily crosses up of them. The piano vamps continue beneath dialogue.)

GRIEVER: The unconscious.
BOO: Yes?
GRIEVER: The human being's unconscious?
BOO: Yes?
GRIEVER: All right. I have been in therapy for about seventy-five years.

(Freeze.)

EMILY *(Sings)*:

    I came to the city
    To get away from Mother.
    Some of you others
    Are here for the same reason.
    Worked as a file clerk.
    Met a man and fell in love.
    He told me he was married.
    I thought it didn't matter.
    We took an apartment.
    Lived there for nearly half a year.
    He said he'd divorce his wife.
    I couldn't tell my mother.
    One night I left him,
    Left him in that apartment.
    All my books and records,
    Well, I suppose they're still there.

(Unfreeze. Vamp continues.)

GRIEVER: And—
ALICE: You're going to have a breakthrough any day now.
GRIEVER: Thanks. No, I really have thought about this. Do . . . ?

(Freeze. Emily has crossed up of Griever.)

EMILY *(Sings)*:

    Uptown
    Found a place with two roommates.
    We all work in offices.
    I found a new boyfriend.
    Some weekends
    He takes me to the country
    Where he gives his wild parties.
    Those nights I sleep alone.
    And I'm weary,

Tired of turning on
With so many people
With nothing in their faces.
From California
To Mississippi
Everybody's looking
For just the same thing.

(Unfreeze. Music slowly fades out under dialogue.)

GRIEVER: Do patients—? What am I trying to say? Does everybody—? Everybody has an unconscious.

ALICE: Presumably.

GRIEVER: Does everybody have the same— *(To Emily)* This is going to sound so stupid— *(To Boo)* basically the same kinds of—

BOO: Yes, I think so.

(Emily sits.)

ALICE: He hasn't even asked the question.

BOO: I know. I think I know what he's getting at—

GRIEVER *(Simultaneously)*: I mean, I see people on the street, all right?

BOO: Uh-huh?

GRIEVER: Politicians.

BOO: Yes, I think it's natural to wonder about—and I think the answer is yes.

ALICE: To what? What's the question?

BOO: People's basic fears and basic inner mechanisms are the same, is that what you're asking?

GRIEVER: Yeah. Sort of. Is it? I don't know.

ALICE *(Overlapping)*: But you don't know that.

BOO: No, I don't. He asked what I thought. I think the differences between people are superficial and—

ALICE: But—

BOO: Basically—basically we're all cut from the same cloth.

GRIEVER: All right, but . . . I mean, okay, why does somebody become a Nazi?

ALICE *(Under Boo and Griever)*: What was I just reading? . . . God, it was this incredible quote . . . This is—this is exactly what it was about . . . What the fuck was that—?

BOO: Well, it's—I mean, the Marxists—

GRIEVER: Right—

BOO: —say it's economic, the Freudians say it's because the Germans toilet-train their kids too soon.

GRIEVER: Right, the whole tie between—

BOO: Sadism—

GRIEVER: Right.

TOM: Because they what?

BOO: They toilet-train their kids too soon.

TOM: So they killed six million Jews?

BOO: It's really not as stupid as it sounds—

ALICE *(Simultaneously)*: But—may I say something? I don't see—I mean, a child's experience isn't the same as an adult's. A woman's—I don't know what a penis feels like.

BOO: That's not the question.

ALICE: I mean, I know what one feels like, but—

GRIEVER *(Simultaneously)*: Alice! Alice, Alice, Alice.

ALICE: Why do we have to have I'm-the-same-as-you, you're-the-same-as-me? Why does one person scream when they get a hangnail and another person not even flinch when they get—

BOO *(Overlapping)*: Because. You know why.

ALICE: Why?

BOO: Because they're sissies.

NORBERT: Okay. Did you ever wonder—as a kid—if what you saw as the color blue—

ALICE: Yes! Yes, that's what I'm saying!

NORBERT *(Overlapping)*: —and what other people saw as the color blue was really like two different colors?

BOO: But it's not.

ALICE: You don't know that.

BOO: I do know it. Physiologically it's the same.

ALICE: But you're not inside his experience.

BOO: True, I am deducing it's the same.

ALICE: Empirically?

BOO: Not empirically.

ALICE *(Not stopping, to Emily)*: I have no idea what that word means, do you? No, you can go sit where Norbert sits, but you won't see what Norbert sees.

GRIEVER: Well, Norbert won't see anything if she's sitting in his lap—

ALICE *(Overlapping)*: No, all right, if this were a play?

BOO *(Overlapping)*: May I just interject something here?

ALICE: What?

BOO: I really love this punch.

ALICE: Good.

BOO: I would like to get in the bowl and go for a swim.

ALICE: If this were a play or a novel?

EMILY: Uh-huh?

BOO *(Crossing to the bar)*: I would like to have a relationship with this punch . . . Raise little baby punch bowls . . .

ALICE *(Overlapping)*: You have the whole web of connections: how you know Libby and why you're here and what I know about you and what you know about me, but even if you could graph it all out?

GRIEVER *(Overlapping; to Boo)*: Thank you for sharing that . . .

NORBERT: Yeah?

ALICE: Even if you could put all the different pieces of the puzzle together, your piece and my piece and—

GRIEVER: Watch it, Al.

ALICE: Right. And what you want and why you say what you say or don't say and what's going on in the kitchen and what you did this afternoon and what I'm going to do when I get home and what he's thinking—even if you could assemble all these little pieces of the puzzle—

GRIEVER: Right.

ALICE: From all the different angles so they all fit together perfectly . . .

EMILY: Uh-huh?

ALICE: You would still have . . . a puzzle.

(No reaction.)

I thought that was so brilliant.

(Libby has just entered.)

LIBBY: Food's almost ready.
ALICE: All right, here's Libby.
GRIEVER: Heeeeeeeeeeeeeeeeere's Libby!

(Griever, Tom and Boo all sing the Johnny Carson theme. Alice barrels ahead.)

ALICE: All right, I promise I'll shut up as soon as I finish this. Do you mind my using you as an example?
LIBBY: No.
ALICE: Even if you could ascertain why Libby—wants to go skydiving or why she had us all here for dinner or why, I don't know, she wears her hair like that or why her lip itches, you still couldn't—

(Griever has stifled a laugh.)

What?
LIBBY: Nothing.
ALICE: You still couldn't feel the itch.
GRIEVER: Oh go ahead, tell 'em.
ALICE: The defense rests, I'm sorry.
LIBBY *(Overlapping; under her breath)*: Griever!
GRIEVER: Go on.
ALICE: What?
GRIEVER: Nobody cares.
ALICE: What?
LIBBY: I don't want to.
GRIEVER: You're being silly.
LIBBY: That's my prerogative, isn't it?

(Long pause. Everyone stares at her. At last she gives in, smiles a big toothy grin.)

Hi.

(Lights dim to scene-change light; at the same time the soprano aria "Doretta's Dream" from Puccini's La Rondine is heard, full volume. The actors again rearrange the black sculptural pieces; this time they all face full front. Alice and Boo will be center stage; Libby and Norbert stage right; Tom and Emily stage left; Griever alone upstage, his back to the audience.)

SCENE 3

Libby and Norbert are clearing away dishes. Griever sits motionless, alone. Emily, wearing Tom's long shirt and nothing else, is eating popcorn and watching television, the sound turned off. Alice and Boo are listening to the aria out of the scene change. Deep violet light against the scrim, visible through the window/canvas.

SOPRANO *(Singing)*: Folle amore! Folle ebrazza! Chi la sottil carezza d'un bacio cosi ardente mai ridi potra!
ALICE: Listen.
SOPRANO: Ah! mio sogno!
ALICE *(Spoken)*: Ah! my soul!
SOPRANO: Ah! mia vita!
ALICE: Ah! my life!
SOPRANO: Che importa la richezza se alfine e rigiorita le felicita O sogno d'or poter amar . . .
BOO: It's beautiful.

(Boo puts on her headphones and resumes language lesson from Scene 1. Alice gets up and turns off the music, offstage. Libby reenters, to see Norbert collecting more dirty dishes.)

LIBBY: Oh, just leave those.
NORBERT: I don't mind.

LIBBY: All right.

(Norbert exits with dishes; Libby sits.)

TOM *(Entering, shirt open)*: Fucking dykes, you know?

ALICE *(Reentering)*: Everybody seemed nice, I thought.

BOO: What?

ALICE: Oh, sorry.

BOO: No, say.

ALICE: I said I thought everybody seemed nice, didn't you?

BOO: Mmmmm.

ALICE: You don't have to use the headphones.

BOO: No, they help.

ALICE: Oh.

TOM *(Continuing; under Alice and Boo)*: The trouble with Shakespeare, of course, is the same thing that's wrong with Beethoven and Bach, basically . . . ya-da ya-da . . . Turn the sound up.

EMILY: No, I like to try to figure out what they're saying.

TOM: Yeah? Make up stories? I used to do that when I was a kid. Sneak down and watch TV at night without the sound, try to imagine what the story was. Give everybody names.

(Norbert reenters.)

And then something would happen in the story that didn't make sense with what I'd already decided and I'd have to shift everything around. Readjust my prejudices. My alliances.

EMILY: Uh-huh.

NORBERT: Do you want to be alone or something?

LIBBY: No, actually, I don't.

ALICE: I'm tired.

NORBERT: All right. *(He exits with more dishes)*

ALICE: Do you mind if I put my head in your lap? *(She does)* Mmmmmm. *(Pause; says an Italian word she likes)* Montagne.

BOO: Hm?

ALICE: Montagne.

BOO: What do I say?

ALICE: I don't know.

TOM *(Overlapping)*: . . . Fucking song . . . *(Picks up his sheet music, resumes work)*

BOO: Montagne.

ALICE: Montagne.

BOO: Montagne.

LIBBY *(Calling offstage)*: That's enough.

BOO *(Deliberately mispronouncing)*: Mon-tag-nee.

NORBERT *(Reentering)*: I just want you to know I'm a world-renowned, championship dishwasher.

LIBBY: Well, I don't care, Norbert, I want you to sit down right now and be nice to me.

NORBERT: Do I have to?

TOM: I mean, I know—I *know* I can write it, I just can't write it. You know?

NORBERT: So.

TOM: I know just what it should be, I can hear it.

NORBERT: Tell me about yourself . . .

TOM *(Continuing)*: I can feel what the words are, I just can't . . .

NORBERT: How's that for a first line?

TOM *(Very soft)*: It's like one of those fucking jingles that goes around in your head, you know?

LIBBY *(Overlapping)*: Well . . . I have no tooth.

NORBERT: Uh-huh?

LIBBY: And beyond that . . .

EMILY *(Simultaneously)*: Uh-huh?

TOM: I just can't . . . I almost asked everybody to shut up for a second, I was like afraid I was going to lose it.

EMILY: What, at the party?

NORBERT: So who were all these people?

LIBBY: Tonight? You know, Norb?

TOM *(Looking at the sheet music)*: I don't know . . .

LIBBY: I really don't know.

TOM: I don't know about the middle part.

LIBBY: I really don't.

NORBERT: Weren't they your friends?

TOM: Which sounds better? *(He picks up the guitar, plays)*

NORBERT: What?

ALICE *(Simultaneously)*: What?

BOO: Hm?

ALICE: What are you thinking?

LIBBY: I'm not being very good company, am I?

NORBERT: It's okay.

LIBBY: Is it?

BOO *(Overlapping)*: What do you suppose Libby's story is?

ALICE: She's straight, I'm sure.

BOO: Nooooooo.

LIBBY: I'm glad.

ALICE: Oh, I don't know, what do you mean? . . . You have that look on your face.

LIBBY: I like you.

BOO: I don't know . . .

NORBERT: I like you too.

BOO: I can't put my finger on it.

ALICE: Did you want to put your finger on it? What about Griever, is he straight?

BOO: Why does everything always have to come back to us?

ALICE: It doesn't—it doesn't, I'm just curious.

TOM: Or. *(Plays another version of the same phrase)*

LIBBY: Music?

ALICE: What about Emily?

BOO: She's straight.

LIBBY: Or something to drink?

BOO: No, I liked her.

ALICE: You did?

LIBBY *(Simultaneously)*: Easy to please, aren't you?

BOO: Mm-hm.

ALICE: Me too. Maybe a little bimbotic, but . . .

BOO: What?

ALICE: Bimbotic? The adjective form of bimbo?

BOO: Bimbotic?

ALICE: You like that?

TOM *(Simultaneously)*: Wait, I'll play 'em again. *(He does)*

BOO: Did you make that up?

ALICE: I don't know. Maybe.

BOO: You don't know if you made it up?

NORBERT: Can I ask you something?

LIBBY: Sure.

NORBERT: It's none of my business, but . . . are you and Griever—?

LIBBY: Oh. No. Sort of. Who knows?

NORBERT: Uh-huh.

TOM: That's one, all right?

LIBBY: I don't know what we are. He's helped me a lot, and I love him, but . . . it's not really—I'm not really ready. He is. I'm not. I'd like to be.

NORBERT: Uh-huh.

LIBBY: Not necessarily for Griever. I don't know what I mean. Sorry.

NORBERT: That's okay.

TOM *(Finishes playing)*: That's the other one. What do you think?

EMILY: Well. They sound sort of the same. Sorry.

LIBBY: Sorry.

ALICE *(Sitting up)*: Sorry.

NORBERT: No.

BOO: What's the matter?

ALICE: I drank too much.

BOO: What?

ALICE *(Exiting)*: I drank too much.

> *(Griever has gotten up and dialed his phone. Libby's phone rings. She looks at it. It rings again.)*

NORBERT: You want me to get it?

> *(Libby shakes her head, goes to phone, answers.)*

LIBBY: Hi.

GRIEVER: Congratulations, congratulations!

LIBBY: Thanks.

GRIEVER *(Singing)*: Bum-ba-bum-bum-bum-bum-bum!

LIBBY: Thanks.

GRIEVER: You did it.

LIBBY: Wellll—

GRIEVER: You did, come on.

LIBBY: Yeah. Everybody left kind of early.

GRIEVER: Early? It's eleven o'clock on Sunday night.

LIBBY: Yeah, I know.

GRIEVER: It was terrific, it really was. I'm real proud of you. You're over the hump.

LIBBY: I guess.

GRIEVER: You are. I think it was terrific, I really do. Alice is a stitch, isn't she?

LIBBY: Isn't she?

GRIEVER: And Boo? Tom seemed to have a good time.

LIBBY: Oh good, I couldn't tell.

GRIEVER: You by yourself?

LIBBY: You should have stayed, you just flew out the door.

GRIEVER: I know, I know.

LIBBY: You home?

GRIEVER: Is Norbert still there?

LIBBY: We were just sitting and talking a bit—

GRIEVER: Uh-huh.

LIBBY: Relaxing. Did you get a cab?

GRIEVER: Oh yeah, no problem, but listen, I'll let you go.

LIBBY: Please don't—

GRIEVER: No, I'm a jerk.

LIBBY: You're not a jerk, you're terrific.

GRIEVER: I'll see you in group, all right? *(He hangs up, takes his phone off the hook)*

LIBBY: Grieve? *(To Norbert)* I'll just be a second. *(She dials, listens, hangs up)*

NORBERT: Listen, maybe . . .

LIBBY: No, please, I like having you here. Please stay.

NORBERT: Okay.

(They sit.)

LIBBY: Oh, Norbert.
NORBERT: What?
LIBBY: You're so sweet and you have such a stupid name.
NORBERT: Thanks.
LIBBY: I don't know.
NORBERT: Well first thing, we've got to get you a dentist.

(Libby laughs hysterically.)

What? . . . What? . . .

(Her laugh goes on and on, verging on the hysterical.)

LIBBY: I'm sorry.
NORBERT: What did I say?

(She looks as if she may be crying.)

Hey.
LIBBY: Oh God.
NORBERT: Hey.
LIBBY: I'm sorry.
NORBERT: Don't be sorry. I'm right here.
LIBBY: Oh . . .
NORBERT: Come on.
LIBBY: I can't, I'm sorry.
NORBERT: That's okay.
LIBBY: No, it's not you.
NORBERT: I know.
BOO *(Having taken off her headphones, she calls to offstage)*:
     Are you all right?
LIBBY: I'm sorry.
BOO: Baby?
ALICE *(From off)*: I'm fine, I'm sitting on the pot.
BOO: All right.
NORBERT: All right?
TOM: What's happening?

EMILY *(Staring at the television)*: I can't tell yet. Somebody's trying to get something from somebody.

TOM: Like what?

EMILY: I can't tell. You have to watch.

LIBBY: . . . When I first came to New York?

NORBERT: Uh-huh?

(Griever, who has remained standing, smoking a cigarette, now places the receiver back in its cradle and sits on the back of his armchair, his back to the audience. Boo is lying on her side, resting on her elbow. Tom continues work on his song. Emily never takes her eyes off the television screen.)

LIBBY: I didn't know a soul, you know? I didn't know why I was here or what I was going to do. I just came.

NORBERT: Uh-huh.

LIBBY: And I ran into Tom on the street.

NORBERT: Uh-huh.

LIBBY: It was nice, you now, to see a familiar face even though we weren't all that close in high school. And we started messing around. Nothing serious, it was never anything serious . . . Then I went to get my teeth cleaned, of all things. I had thirteen cavities, so I wound up . . . seeing a lot of . . .

NORBERT: The—

LIBBY: The dentist. Right. You got it. And . . . Martin Vanderhoffer.

NORBERT: Uh-huh.

LIBBY: And he was just a lot of fun. His family had a lot of money. I mean, a lot of money, so he didn't have to work at all if he didn't want to, but he liked to which I liked. And he was fun.

NORBERT: Uh-huh.

LIBBY: And so we started to go out. And I didn't see Tom much. At all. And I got more involved with Marty. We talked about getting married . . .

ALICE *(From off)*: I know what I wanted to show you.

BOO: What?

ALICE: I remembered what I wanted to show you, if I can find it.

BOO: What?

LIBBY *(Overlapping)*: Aaaaand we did. Get married.

NORBERT: Uh-huh.

LIBBY: Big wedding. And . . . we laughed. Marty . . . We bought a big apartment on East 71st Street—much too big for just the two of us. Brand-new building, we had a terrace and windows on three sides. It was almost the penthouse. We'd been married about three months—not quite—. And . . . I think I was pregnant. I was. We talked about it and I was late. Anyway, I could have been . . . And we were standing by the window. I didn't have any clothes on. I was looking out. It was late—late afternoon. Everything was blue—as blue as it can be before it gets black.

NORBERT: Uh-huh?

LIBBY: And Marty said, Come out on the terrace. I said, I don't have any clothes on. And he brought me this little robe. And we walked out on the terrace.

(Boo puts her hand over her eyes as if she has a headache.)

We'd only lived there two months. And he kissed me and I put my head back to look up at the sky. Our reflections were in the glass. And I put my head back; we lived on the seventh floor, there was another above us.

(Griever puts his head back as if sighing.)

And we leaned—he leaned—I set my back against the rail and it . . . just . . . We were gone; we were over. I saw us leave the window. I looked—past him, my hands reached past him to try to hold something, there wasn't anything . . . just blue . . . And I didn't black out. I thought—very clearly . . . This is bad. This is real. And it's true, you see everything pass before your eyes. Everything. Slowly, like a dream, and Marty was . . .

Marty was climbing up me and screaming and we turned . . . over . . . once . . . and . . . we went through an awning . . . Sloan's . . . Which saved my life . . . And I broke every bone in my face. I have a completely new face. My teeth were all shattered; these are all caps.

ALICE *(From off)*: Now I know this is here because I just saw it.

BOO: What?

ALICE: Wait.

LIBBY: I was in traction for ten months. And Tom came to see me every week. Every day sometimes. Marty's family. Who sued the building. I mean, they never even attached it to the wall. It wasn't even attached. It was just a rail—a loose rail. There was another one on another floor, the same thing could have happened . . . I landed on him. I killed him. I can't—

(Norbert moves toward her; she flinches.)

It's seven years. I'm thirty-three years old. I can't have anybody hold me. I can never be held.

(Pause.)

NORBERT: I'm going to stay here, all right? . . . I won't hold you . . .

(Alice comes on with a book.)

BOO: What is this?

ALICE *(Reading)*: "There is, let us confess it . . ." Wait.

(She sits next to Boo, who is sitting up again.)

BOO: Who is this?

ALICE: "About sympathy—" All right, just listen.

NORBERT: All right?

ALICE *(Reading)*: "About sympathy, for example. We can do without it. That illusion of a world so shaped that it echoes every groan, of human beings so tied together by common needs and fears that a twitch at one wrist jerks another, where however strange your experience other people have had it too, where however far you travel in your own mind a someone has been there before you—is all an illusion."

BOO: Who is this?

ALICE: "We do not know our own souls, let alone the souls of others. Human beings do not go hand in hand the whole stretch of the way. There is no virgin forest in each; a snowfield where even the print of birds' feet is unknown." . . . *Collected Essays, Volume Four*, V. Woolf. *(She puts down the book)* What's the matter?

NORBERT: It's going to be all right.

BOO: Do you even love me?

ALICE: Of course I love you. Honey. I love you so very much, you know that.

(Griever dials Libby's number and hangs up before it can ring.)

BOO: You know, if you'd said "I love you so much" or "I love you very much" but you love me "so very much"?

ALICE: What's wrong with that?

BOO: What is that? Who is that for?

ALICE: I don't understand, I really don't.

BOO: I think you're more in love with the sound of your own voice than you are with me is what I think.

ALICE: Why? Because I read a passage from Virginia Woolf?

BOO *(Overlapping)*: If you want to know what I think—. Because you have to be right, Alice. You have to, have to be right. Always. Always, Alice. It's like you don't think I have a brain in my head.

ALICE: I think you're one of the smartest people I ever met in my life.

BOO *(Overlapping)*: But you don't. It's like you made me up in your head. Oh, Alice's lover is a doctor. Isn't that interesting? Isn't that flattering? To Alice.

TOM: This fucking . . .

BOO *(Overlapping)*: You ask me questions about things I know about—science—and then you answer your own question. Incorrectly.

TOM *(Overlapping)*: . . . I know what it is . . . I know it . . .

ALICE: What are we talking about? The corpus callosum? I was just so pleased I remembered.

BOO: You're always so pleased. You're always so pleased with yourself.

ALICE: Well, what? Empirical? I was playing—

BOO *(Overlapping)*: It's not that.

ALICE: Honey, I absolutely adore you and if I'm not communicating it—

BOO *(Overlapping)*: It's not that.

TOM: That's it. All right.

ALICE: Then tell me what it is, all right?

(Griever dials.)

TOM: All *right*.

ALICE: What? . . . Please.

(Libby's phone rings.)

BOO: I miss . . .

(Ring.)

NORBERT: I'll get it.

TOM: I got it. Finally.

NORBERT *(After the second ring)*: Hello?

ALICE: What?

NORBERT: Hello?

BOO: I miss us.

(Griever hangs up.)

ALICE: Us?

NORBERT: Hung up.

BOO: I miss our time together.

ALICE: We're going away in three weeks.

BOO: I miss . . . The first time you made love to me? I felt like a baby being born.

(Tom plays the guitar, softly.)

And now . . . I'll never forget when you first touched me.

(Emily has switched off the TV and is staring into space.)

TOM: You all right?

BOO: At Carl's? I'll never forget that feeling.

EMILY: You know what I wish?

BOO: Oh my god. Falling in love with you?

TOM *(Simultaneously)*: Wait, baby, I'm almost finished.

BOO *(Continuing)*: November? And moving in here with you. And now I'm always on call. And your damn book, I hate that book, I do.

ALICE: I know.

BOO: I do. I don't care what you call it, pick something. Call it *Poop on Ice*. I'm tired of hearing little bits of it and should his name be Frank or should it be Franklin? I listen to people all day long, I listen to their problems, I listen to their little—

TOM: I've almost got it.

BOO: —niggling fucking complaints about nothing—

ALICE: I know, I know—

BOO: —and none of them ever gets any better.

ALICE: That's not true.

BOO: And it's not going to be any better even if I start a private practice, it's always going to be other people's problems as long as I live.

ALICE: That's the work you chose.

TOM *(Sings)*: "From California to Mississippi . . ." Mmmm. *(Finishes the song, satisfied)* All right, what do you wish?

LIBBY: I wish . . .

EMILY: I wish everybody had a little window. Right in front like a TV screen?

LIBBY: Sometimes I wish . . .

TOM: A window?

EMILY: You know. Like just a little window where you could see in and see what they were feeling and thinking about.

LIBBY: I don't know . . .

EMILY: So you wouldn't always have to wonder. You could just see. Wouldn't that be neat?

LIBBY: We would be by the window. You know? And Marty would say, Come out on the terrace. And I'd say, . . . No. Let's stay here.

ALICE: Baby.

LIBBY: It's so blue.

ALICE: I'm here.

LIBBY: All right?

TOM: Well, I wish we had a piano is what I wish.

LIBBY: Oh God.

NORBERT: It's all right.

TOM: You know?

LIBBY: God.

NORBERT: It's all right.

TOM: Big . . . black . . . baby grand . . . Sit her in the window?

BOO: I wish we were there right now.

TOM: All that light?

BOO: I do.

TOM: Blue light? You know?

BOO: I just want to walk on the Grand Canal with you.

TOM: Cold . . . white . . . keys . . .

BOO: And hold your hand.

TOM: Smooth, clean.

BOO *(Beginning to overlap)*: And make love to you.

TOM: God.

ALICE: Cara mia.

BOO: I do.

TOM: I can just feel it.

ALICE: Come la nascita d'una bambina.

BOO: What's that?

ALICE: Like a baby being born.

(As they all begin to speak together, no voice can take more importance than another. They are all quiet and distinct— taking their time.)

LIBBY: We would just be by the window . . . And I would say . . . stay with me here . . . It's so blue . . . Stay here . . .

EMILY *(Overlapping)*: I really do . . . And you could crawl right in. Like . . . if everyone was made of glass. I would love that . . .

BOO *(Overlapping)*: I wish we were there . . . Right now . . . And I could fall in love with you again—. All over again, but this time in Venice—

TOM *(Overlapping)*: Just touch the keys, you know? And—

(Tom reaches forward as if to play the piano. He presses his finger down and we hear the song he has been trying to write, the piano accompaniment to Emily's song, very soft at first.)

Damn!

NORBERT: I know.

EMILY: If you could just open up the window and crawl in . . .

ALICE *(Overlapping)*: Ti adoro . . .

LIBBY *(Overlapping)*: And we would just . . . We would just float away . . .

BOO *(Overlapping)*: And we could look in all the windows . . . Hold hands . . . Everything'll be blue . . .

(Griever sways to the music very gently.)

LIBBY *(Overlapping)*: We would become the blue . . . Just the two of us . . . You know? . . .

EMILY *(Overlapping)*: I do . . . I wish everyone was made of glass. And I wish everybody had a little window. Don't you? . . . I do . . .

ALICE *(Overlapping)*: Ti amo.

BOO *(Overlapping)*: And we'll ride in the gondola? And we'll just float away . . .

LIBBY *(Overlapping)*: Right through the glass . . . We would just . . . float . . . away . . .

ALICE *(Overlapping)*: Come la nascita d'una bambina . . .

LIBBY *(Overlapping)*: Right through the glass . . .

BOO: Okay? We'll just . . . float away . . .

LIBBY: Forever . . .

> *(The music becomes rhapsodic. With an invisible partner, Griever dances among the three couples, ending his dance at the canvas, facing away from us, as the lights fade.)*

END OF PLAY

STRANGER

■ *For John Bartholomew McDermott* ■

Stranger premiered at the Vineyard Theatre (Douglas Aibel, Artistic Director; Bardo S. Ramirez, Managing Director) in New York City on October 17, 2000. The director was Mark Brokaw. Set design was by Neil Patel, costume design was by Jess Goldstein, lighting design was by Mark McCullough, original music and sound design were by David Van Tieghem and Jill B.C. DuBoff and the stage manager was Katherine Lee Boyer. The cast was as follows:

LINDA	Kyra Sedgwick
HUSH	David Strathairn
STEWARD/FRANK/PATO/CAPTAIN	David Harbour
STEWARDESS/LINDA'S MOM/DIANE	Julianne Nicholson

HUSH

forties

LINDA

thirties

STEWARDESS

also plays Linda's Mom and Diane

STEWARD

also plays Frank, Pato and the Voice of the Captain

■ TIME AND PLACE ■

Stranger takes place on a flight from Philadelphia to Seattle and in a remote cabin in the Pacific Northwest. Other scenes, remembered, are also seen—an apartment in Portland, Oregon; a cabin in Coburn, Pennsylvania; and a jail cell in Carlisle, Pennsylvania.

■ ABOUT THE TEXT ■

Any dialogue appearing in brackets is unspoken. A comma that may seem incorrect or unnecessary signifies a tiny pause or switch in the character's thinking.

Now we pay forfeit on old abdications
The child dares flames his father lit
And in the briefness of too bright flames
Shrivels a heritage of blighted futures

—WOLE SOYINKA

Have I told you no life is the same?

—ANTHONY LA BARCA FALCONE
Otisville Correctional Facility
Otisville, New York, 1996

I hate and I love. And if you ask me how, I do not know.
I only feel it, and I'm torn in two.

—CATULLUS
Translated by Peter Whigham

Two adjacent airline seats. Hush enters.

STEWARDESS *(Over speaker)*: . . . if you have brought on two carry-on items, we ask that you place one under the seat in front of you. For those customers seated in the first row of each cabin, carry-on items may not be placed on the floor against the cabin divider partition. If you need help locating a place for your carry-on luggage, please ask one of the flight attendants.

STEWARD *(Entering)*: Yes?

HUSH: Am I in the right seat? The travel agent told me I had a window seat.

STEWARD: Maybe your seatmate will switch with you.

HUSH: No, it isn't that, I just don't want to . . .

STEWARD: You're fine.

(Steward moves off. Hush reads his Bible. Linda enters.)

LINDA: I'm . . .

(Linda sits next to Hush.)

STEWARDESS *(Over speaker)*: Our flight cannot leave the gate until your carry-on items have been put away, all overhead bins have been closed, and all passengers are seated. Customers seated in an exit row may need to open that exit in the event of an emergency. Please review the Safety Briefing Card in the—

LINDA: Is there a living person who hasn't already memorized this thing?

STEWARDESS *(Under, continuous)*: —seat pocket in front of you, then contact a flight—

LINDA: Be quiet!

STEWARDESS: —attendant if you cannot or do not wish to operate the exit. Cellular phones can interfere with aircraft systems and therefore may not be used on board the aircraft at any time, including at the gate. All electronic devices must be turned off and put away at this time. Please unplug any devices that are plugged into the seat power outlets. After takeoff, we'll let you know when you may use them and also remind you when they should be turned off and put away for landing. Also for your safety, please be careful when opening overhead bins as objects may have shifted in flight. Please direct your attention to the flight attendants in your cabin as they demonstrate the safety features of our F-737 aircraft.

(The Stewardess's voice continues under Linda and Hush.)

LINDA: I *hate* to fly. Oh god. We're in an exit row. Well, if we have a water landing— That always cracks me up, *water landing*: "Wheee, mommy!, we're having a water landing!" Right? Well, I'll just, uh . . . You can take over the

STEWARDESS: To fasten your seat belt, insert the metal fitting into the buckle, then pull the loose end to tighten the belt. To unfasten your seat belt, lift the top portion of the buckle. Your seat belt should remain fastened at all times. As we prepare for

LINDA *(continued)*:
    exit door duties, okay? . . .
    Deal. I'm Linda.
HUSH: Hush.
LINDA: . . . Okay.

HUSH: No, that's my name,
    everyone does that.

LINDA: Hush? Is your name?
    Did your parents? . . .
    I mean . . . I don't know . . .
    Did they just *want* you to
    turn out like somebody
    who gets into fights in
    bars? I mean . . . It's . . .
    an explicit criticism of
    everyone else, isn't it?

STEWARDESS *(continued)*:
    takeoff, please be sure
    your seat backs are
    straight up, tray tables
    are put away and carry-on
    luggage is placed
    under the seat in front
    of you. There is no
    smoking on this flight.
    Federal law prohibits
    tampering with, disabling,
    or destroying smoke
    detectors in the lavatories.
    There are two clearly
    marked exit doors at each
    end of the airplane and
    window exits over the
    wings. In the event of a
    power loss—

CAPTAIN *(Over speaker)*: Flight attendants prepare for take-
off.
LINDA: Oh boy ohboyohboyohboyoh—
HUSH: It's okay.
LINDA: I mean . . .
HUSH: Relax.
LINDA: Don't you hate when you open a book on a plane
and the person next to you just starts telling you about
their life or the most recent book *they've* read. If I start
screaming just put your hand over my mouth, okay?
HUSH: You're doing fine.
LINDA: Okayyyyy, just floating over the world, high high
above the world, in a fifty-five-million-ton . . . vehicle
which floats by . . . sommmmme invisible means and
never never never thinks twice about how it stays up
here. And there it is, the world. Tiny and unreal, beautiful, clean, perfect. *(Short pause)* Trade with me,
would you?

HUSH: Sure.

LINDA: Thank you.

STEWARDESS *(Over speaker)*: Ladies and gentlemen, please remain seated until the captain has turned off the overhead seat belt sign.

LINDA: I'll look at this beauuuuuutiful carpet over here, this lovely indoor-outdoor . . .

HUSH: The Lord doesn't give us anything we can't handle.

LINDA: Are you talking about me or . . . ?

HUSH: Fear. Your f—

LINDA: "The Nightmare Seatmate."

HUSH: He doesn't.

(He moves his bag out of Linda's way.)

Here, let me—

LINDA: It's fine. Thanks. *(Pause)* My boyfriend would never do that. Move it. I would actually have to say, Frank, your bag is on my side, there's no room for my things, and then he would, but the idea . . . He's like my father's generation, I mean, he's not that old, he's my age, but he has . . . you know, that post-war thing that men had which is whatever the woman wants, he can't make up his mind, I mean, he has no . . . apparent desires, it's all about what I want. I think underneath what it is is that he is too afraid to even ask himself who he is, what he wants. Where we get this insane idea about men and women; I guess men are good in battle because they're good at taking orders. And honestly? I don't want to give him orders, I don't. What I want, secretly, is to be told

what to do, and I am only telling you that because you are a complete stranger and when we get off this plane I will never see	STEWARDESS *(Over speaker)*: In the event of a power loss, our emergency lighting system will direct you to all exits. Please note the emergency

LINDA *(continued)*:
    you again. If you came
    up to me with a camera
    and a microphone, I
    would say I want equal
    pay for equal work, a
    woman's right to choose,
    and an end to the glass
    ceiling, I'm officially a
    socialist, but . . . you
    know what I'm saying . . .

    Oh, yeah, we'll be
    breathing normally at
    that point—
    Tra la la, here come
    the oxygen masks . . .
    So tell me something.

HUSH: What?

LINDA: No, I mean, anything,
    tell me anything.

HUSH: Oh, well . . . I'm . . .
    just . . . sitting here.

LINDA: I knew that already.
    (Pause)
    All right.
    (Pause)

STEWARDESS *(continued)*:
    exit nearest your seat. If
    there is a sudden change
    in cabin pressure, a mask
    compartment above your
    head will open auto-
    matically. If this happens,
    quickly reach for the
    nearest mask and pull it
    firmly to you; this will
    start the flow of oxygen.
    Please ensure the plastic
    bag is clear of the mask
    and place the yellow cup
    over your nose and mouth
    and continue to breathe
    normally.

    Secure the mask to
    your face with the elastic
    band. It may be
    tightened by
    pulling on the tabs
    located on either side
    of the mask. Even
    though oxygen is flowing,
    the mask may not
    inflate. If you
    are traveling with
    or seated next to a
    child or any person
    who may need
    your assistance,
    put your mask on first
    before helping them.
    Make sure their mask

HUSH: I'm . . . giving my life over to Jesus Christ . . . Moving to a new city where I don't know anybody except a contact at my church . . . I'm hoping to . . . get my own place. And find work, meaning—, some kind of, you know . . . meaningful work.

STEWARDESS *(continued)*: fits tightly to their face. Once we reach our cruising altitude, we will be coming through the aisle with a beverage cart.

LINDA: What would . . . for you, what would be meaningful work?

HUSH: I would like . . . I think I would like to find a way to help people in . . . some of the ways I've been helped.

LINDA: How is that?

HUSH: Finding . . . finding Christ's love. All . . . embracing. All forgiving.

(Short pause.)

LINDA: Have you tried hustling? You could . . . No, I'm sorry, that was terrible, I'm really . . . I think it's wonderful you . . . found something. "All embracing," I just thought . . . That was stupid. What kind of work did you, do you do now?

HUSH: Oh, I . . . That's okay. We all have that little voice that says, that's embarrassed by love, by God. I used to work cleaning pools, for a guy who had a company cleaning pools—

LINDA: Uh-huh.

HUSH: You know, in the summer, when . . .

LINDA: Pools are—

HUSH: In the winter I would . . . I'm pretty much a loner. Was.

(Short pause.)

LINDA: You're not anymore?
HUSH: We'll see.

(Pause.)

LINDA: Great.
HUSH: I've been incarcerated. For . . .
LINDA: Oh, wow.

(Pause.)

HUSH: Fifteen years.
LINDA: God. Good for you. I mean, for getting out.
HUSH: Thanks.
LINDA: Which was? When?

CAPTAIN (Over speaker):
Ladies and gentle-
men, this is Captain
Wojick speaking.
Now that we have   HUSH: Oh. Today.
reached our cruising
altitude and are   LINDA: Today? Oh. So . . .
forecasting a smooth
flight, I'm about to   HUSH: Yeah.
turn off the seat belt
sign. However, it's   LINDA: God.
best to keep it on in
the event of sudden   HUSH: I know.
turbulence. If you
plan to sleep, please   LINDA: Well. Hello, there!
fasten your seat belt   Welcome to the living.
on the outside of   HUSH: Thanks.
your blanket or jacket
so we won't have   LINDA: You must be . . . Wow.
to disturb you.
And enjoy your flight.   HUSH: Yeah.

LINDA: I'm honored.

HUSH: Most people . . . Thanks. Most people . . . I imagine most people would find that . . .

LINDA: What, that you're out of prison? Scary?

HUSH: Uh-huh.

LINDA: What's gonna happen, we're on a plane, it's not like . . . Good for you.

(Pause.)

Did . . . I mean, did they like teach you skills in prison? Worka[ble]—?

HUSH: Skills?

LINDA: Things you could . . .

HUSH: Mmmm, not skills you'd want anybody to know about.

LINDA: I don't even know what that means, but it sounds . . . It sounds *good*, whatever it means.

HUSH: I found . . . I found God's grace finally. All things in their own time. Jesus isn't on a time schedule.

LINDA: He's probably running this airline then.

(Chime.)

STEWARDESS *(Over speaker)*: Ladies and gentlemen, though the captain has turned off the seat belt sign—

LINDA: We know! . . . Sorry.

STEWARDESS *(Under, continuous)*: —while seated you should keep your seat belt fastened.

LINDA: I had an uncle who went to prison—

HUSH: Oh yeah.

LINDA: —and he never came out, he died in prison, they said it was pneumonia, but I think it was AIDS. Is there a lot of AIDS? . . . Well . . . I can't say that. I was going to say now I don't have to feel bad about my . . . life, but—your suffering isn't about me, is it?, even though . . . People are just the most self-centered, don't you

ever just look at the way people are and think, surely
evolution can do better than this. Look at the things
people have done to other— [people.]

HUSH: Evil . . .

LINDA: Yes, evil.

HUSH: . . . That's—

LINDA: Why, everybody always talks about saving mankind,
but my question?, *Why*? What's so great about people?
In today's paper, cops shooting kids for sport! "How
could this happen?" It could happen because people
like to hurt other people.

HUSH: Yes.

LINDA: It feels good. *(Pause)* It's human . . .

HUSH: Well . . .

LINDA: Well, what is it if it isn't human nature?

HUSH: Satan.

LINDA: You're . . . ? Oh, I always forget people believe that.
Okay, sure, Satan, but he's not going away. He's always
been here.

HUSH: Yes. We are fallen.

LINDA: Oh, fallen shmallen, look at us, it's no different than
the Coliseum when they led human beings out to die
at the hands—

HUSH: Yes.

LINDA: The paws, I guess—ha ha ha ha, pass the popcorn.
What is different about that from the evening news,
will someone tell me? Oh dear, massacres! Awful. —
Honey, is there any more beer?

HUSH: Good and evil.

LINDA *(To Steward or Stewardess)*: Could I have a glass of
water please? I mean, other people are not real to us.
Our comfort is real to us.

HUSH: That's . . . I believe that's the Devil.

LINDA: What? When . . .

HUSH: Do unto others as you would have them do unto you.

LINDA: Okay. Then . . . everyone has the Devil in them—

HUSH: Our soul is our own. We must choose. Sin is univer-
sal. Sin is the condition of life, the Devil is always here,

the Devil is real. And you must choose Christ's love over sin. It's as simple as that.

LINDA: Well, if it were as simple as that . . . I've . . . I'm going to tell you something very intimate. Because you're a total stranger and I'll never see you again . . . All right?

HUSH: But . . .

LINDA: What?

HUSH: Go ahead.

LINDA: What?

HUSH: You . . . Something about you.

LINDA: Oh. Everyone says that.

HUSH: Go ahead.

LINDA: I think there's some . . . person, some character on TV—

HUSH: Oh.

LINDA: —who I'm like or something—

HUSH: Uh-huh.

LINDA: —people are always saying, Hey, how ya doing?, I have no idea who they are . . . Did you watch a lot of TV in . . . ? Well, who is she then? I'd love to know.

HUSH: I didn't mean to—

LINDA: That's okay.

LINDA: You were saying . . . the Devil is other people not being real. But what if they are and that's precisely the point. They are perfectly real, and what you want, deep down, what you desire and enjoy . . . is their humiliation. *(To an unseen passenger)* Sorry. *(To Hush)* My voice gets too loud sometimes, tell me if I'm . . . Okay. I don't know what you were in jail for, and I don't want to know, seriously, I'm serious, I don't want to know. But . . . There are lots of people who have done things who *aren't* in jail, people do things all the time and hope . . . I've done things. And I'm getting away with them. So far. Knock . . . whatever this is. There's probably not one single bit of wood on this plane.

HUSH: Superstitions are the Devil, too.

LINDA: I seem to . . . have a lot of Devil qualities today, maybe you want to change seats. But I've done things.

(The Steward or Stewardess brings a glass of water.)

Oh, thank you . . . They usually make you wait for the cart, I like to . . . I don't know, I guess it gives me the sense that my well-being isn't entirely a matter of indifference to them. If I ask for things, special things . . .

HUSH: Do unto others . . .

LINDA: Do unto others . . . That's right. I'm probably going to be a Bible salesman by the time I get off this flight. You're very nice.

HUSH: You, too.

LINDA: Where are you from?

HUSH: Here. There. *(Long pause)* What things have you done?

LINDA: Mmm. *(Short pause)* Okay. I will be in your in-flight entertainment. At any point you want to tell me to hush . . . Is that your real name?

HUSH: Nickname.

LINDA: Uh-huh.

HUSH: That stuck.

LINDA: Okay. So . . . Your parents always telling you to be quiet? . . . Well, if at any—I mean, I can read, so—don't—

HUSH: Hey, when was the last time a woman spoke to me without a gun in her holster—

LINDA: Uh-huh.

HUSH: —or a uniform?

LINDA: Good point.

HUSH: A woman you'd—Long time. Believe me.

LINDA: Okay. I'm gonna take you at your word . . . I grew up in a very liberal, indifferent home. We had money, *piles*, and just about anything I did was okay, Dad and Mom were busy, "progressive" people, they both worked, nannies, I was never spanked, never told where I couldn't go, if I used a bad word I was reasoned with, it wasn't that they didn't love me, I suppose—anyway, blah blah blah, no boundaries.

HUSH: Uh-huh.

LINDA: I have tattoos in a number of peculiar places—I shot heroin, I dropped out of school, lit fires, I ran away.

Everything was fine, I would find myself, they loved me. It was all a distraction from their busy . . . narcissistic, they didn't love anybody and they still don't except their skis, anyway . . . Do unto others. They are who they are.

HUSH: They hurt you.

LINDA: Well . . .

(He reaches to comfort her; she flinches.)

HUSH: It's okay.

LINDA: No. But . . . Yes. So . . . I moved to Portland and refused to take their money, I had to have some boundaries, I tore up the checks and sent them back, waiting, I suppose, for some sign . . . Someone to come and . . . see if I was still alive. Living in a . . . trailer. Every Sunday . . .

(Linda's Mother appears.)

LINDA'S MOTHER: Hi, honey, checking in, Dad sends his love, we're thinking about you, and hoping you're doing okay, you don't have to call back. We're good here. Everything's good. Hope you are too. We love you . . . It's Mom.

(She exits.)

LINDA: Oh, really? I thought it was . . . No idea how I'm making a living, I could be dead. "We're good here. Everything's good. Hope you are too. We love you." I could have just played that same fucking tape, sorry, I mean—

HUSH: It's okay.

LINDA: Maybe you're Amish or something.

HUSH: Pentecostal.

LINDA: . . . Didn't matter, I was invisible, I did not exist, I was like their organic garden and SAVE THE SPOTTED OWL bumper stickers, something to grace their aura,

for their friends—Oh, anyway. I fell in love with, I got
involved with . . .

HUSH: What?

LINDA: I'm just laughing, this is nuts. And so then, Doctor,
I started shtupping my postman.

(Frank appears.)

It's all so ridiculous . . .

HUSH: Frank?

LINDA: Good memory! So—everyday we'd sit and talk—

*(Linda joins Frank in the past, with frequent asides to
Hush in the present. She can remain in the airplane for
portions of this sequence.)*

FRANK: . . . people don't even . . . you know . . . you don't
even . . . see how beautiful a sprinkler is in the sun, it's
just part of the annoyance, stuff you've got to get
around and through . . .

LINDA: But . . . Frank . . .

FRANK: Uh-huh?

LINDA: It rains every day here, no one has sprinklers.

FRANK: Oh, I know.

LINDA: We were in Portland.

FRANK: I know. But . . .

LINDA: I'm teasing you.

FRANK: . . . you're right though. Oh. I'm thinking of some
other world . . . where I grew up.

LINDA: You miss it?

FRANK: Uhn-uhn.

LINDA: No? *(Pause)* Some . . . how 'bout some more juice? . . .
For weeks . . . just that . . . he doesn't make a move, he
lets me call all the shots, on some perverse level he is
my dad, except I guess in my mind a better dad
because at least he's there, you see.

HUSH: Uh-huh.

LINDA: He's in the room with me, listening, making the most extraordinarily banal observations, because he appears to have no will whatsoever, no desires, just . . . being there, talking, or mostly listening, is all that Frank—he expects nothing of himself or life—Frank.

FRANK: Huh?

LINDA: How can you get away with this?

FRANK: What?

LINDA: Sitting here with me everyday.

FRANK: It's lunch.

LINDA: But you don't eat.

FRANK: Food . . .

LINDA: Yes, food.

FRANK: I can take it or leave it.

LINDA: That's Frank, he can take or leave it. So I become obsessed, of course, I come home from my horrible job at the kitchen supply store where I keep getting promoted no matter how much time I take off, how rude I am to the customers, because it's the eighties and the owner wants to fuck me, but do I like him?, no, he has desires, boundaries, I like *Frank*, and so I conspire, well—Hey.

FRANK: Hey.

LINDA: Do you ever do blow? . . . Coke.

FRANK: Oh.

LINDA: What did you think I was talking about?

FRANK: I don't know.

LINDA: God only knows, you would never know, Frank would never know.

(Frank snorts.)

And within minutes, I swear to God—Nothing, the drug released nothing, there was no demon, no fever waiting to break just below the surface, he was just a faster version of Frank.

FRANK: Uh-huh. Yeah . . . Sure.

LINDA: I didn't say anything.

FRANK: You didn't. Yes, you did.

LINDA: What?

FRANK: You said . . . "Water?" You asked.

LINDA: Oh god.

FRANK: And I'd—

LINDA: That—that was—

FRANK: What?

LINDA: No, you were gonna say something.

FRANK: Oh, I'd like some.

LINDA: That . . .

FRANK: Thanks.

LINDA: That was like minutes ago.

FRANK: It was? No, it wasn't.

LINDA: This was the level of our conversation, No, yeah, maybe, what?, I don't know, but I did not give up, because I knew, on some level I knew that Frank wanted to fuck me, he had too, or else . . . why was he there? *(Another day)* So why don't you have a girlfriend?

FRANK: I work.

LINDA: Uh-huhhhhh. Yes, many people do that.

FRANK: I'm tired when I get home.

LINDA: Are you gay? . . . You're not? Are you sure? . . . Well, how come . . . Are we just like friends or . . . ?

FRANK: I thought that's what you wanted.

LINDA: What do you want?

FRANK: I would . . . I would be your . . . I would be your . . .

LINDA: Boyfriend? You can say that in this house, Frank.

FRANK: You would?

LINDA: What?

FRANK: Be my . . .

LINDA: No, you said you.

FRANK: Well, I don't want to . . . I mean . . .

LINDA: Frank.

FRANK: Yes.

(Short pause.)

LINDA: Never mind.

(Pause.)

FRANK: I should go.
LINDA: Frank.
FRANK: Yes?
LINDA: . . . Take all of your clothes off, slowly, in front of me, and then kiss me and lay down with me here and make love to me, don't go back to work, spend the night with me . . . and see how we do . . . *(Pause)* And we did, every single thing I asked for, except of course he couldn't get it up because of the coke, but . . . he got me off just the way I . . . really like, because I told him how, exactly . . . is this embarrassing you? . . . So I was still waiting for Frank to express his wishes, which— *(Later)* —more than anything in the universe would turn me on.
FRANK: It would?
LINDA: Yes.
FRANK: Why?
LINDA: It just would, Frank. Your . . . what *you* want.
FRANK: But . . . I like this just the way it is.

(Pause.)

LINDA: Okay. That's okay. *(Pause)* But if anything . . . ever, you know . . . just flashes through your mind, something you've always wanted, it doesn't have to be sexual, it could . . . it could be . . . nutritional, it could relate to travel, it could . . . Do you have any food preferences?
FRANK: I've . . . thought about becoming a vegetarian.
LINDA: Have you given up meat? You know the answer.
FRANK: I've always wanted . . . I've always wanted to just . . . You know what I want most of all? . . . To not have to ever ask that question. Or have it asked. Just . . .
LINDA: . . . There we have it.
FRANK: . . . be. *(Pause)* Is that bad? I thought women were tired of men ordering them around . . . being made into objects . . . and . . .

LINDA: That doesn't mean they want to be married to . . . robots.

(Pause.)

FRANK: I would marry you.
LINDA: We had just . . . not fucked for the first time, and Frank would marry me. Okay, so:

(Linda's Mother reappears.)

LINDA'S MOTHER: I can't believe it, honey!
LINDA: I know, I know.
LINDA'S MOTHER: You're happy?
LINDA: I'm . . . I'm okay.
LINDA'S MOTHER: What does he do?
LINDA: He's a postman. He has virtually no personality.
LINDA'S MOTHER: Ohhhh.
LINDA: He likes to do the drugs I like, he satisfies my needs . . .
LINDA'S MOTHER: I'm sorry your dad isn't here to get the news.
LINDA: That's her reaction to anything.
LINDA'S MOTHER: Was it festive?
LINDA: At city hall? *(Pause)* Mom?
LINDA'S MOTHER: Yes?
LINDA: There's something I want to say to you . . . It's important.
LINDA'S MOTHER: All right.
LINDA: So I just need to know that you're listening. That you'll hear me . . .
LINDA'S MOTHER: I will.
LINDA: Okay. It's that . . . um . . . It's really hard to say . . . I . . .
LINDA'S MOTHER: Go ahead.

(Pause. Linda hangs up. Linda's Mother disappears.)

LINDA: She did not call me back.

(Hush reaches over to comfort her and again Linda flinches.)

Sorry. Sorry . . . Frank and I tried all the different drugs, he would find some source, if *I* said I wanted it, he would go into hell and bring back Satan, your friend, but . . . and we'd watch sports on TV, any sport, it didn't matter, hockey is good for coke, baseball is good for acid, soccer is ecstasy, we didn't care who won, we learned all the names of all the players, golf is heroin. Clearly.

(Another day.)

FRANK: You want to know a secret? *(Pause)* I'm gonna be a millionaire. *(Pause)* I am.
LINDA: Yeah? I like that. Positive thinking.
FRANK: No! My grandfather picked me over both my brother and my sister; he had this thing for me, I was special; it's in trust, so I don't spend it all before I'm too old, I mean, I don't spend it all—
LINDA: Right.
FRANK: —before I know how to invest it wisely. So I get it when I'm thirty-five.

(Pause.)

LINDA: Right.
FRANK: I'm serious. *(Short pause)* I didn't want you to know before we were married. I'll show you the papers. I have accountants and people who manage it, here, look . . .
LINDA: And here the great mandala turns, the planets align, and everything . . . is suddenly:

(Frank shows her the papers.)

Cool. Well, what's money . . . finally?

(Short pause.)

FRANK: I know.

LINDA: Well, I'm glad we won't be poor when we're old. You're a very private guy, Frankster. Nowhere as private as I became. You should take up poker. Five years, waiting. Or mortuary science. *(Pause)* Now: the thing with drugs is you have to be stronger than the drug, if you're not, you can't do drugs, because they will take hold of you. Coke, crack and heroin and all the downers and speed are all bad drugs, they close things down. All the hallucinogens are good drugs, they open doors, you see things more clearly, so . . . I would take these, and I wouldn't tell Frank, and I would give him more and more downers and tell him that's what I was taking, too . . . But you have to be very careful, because the thing about the good drugs is they make you want to tell the truth . . .

(Another day.)

You're home early.

FRANK: What are you doing? . . . Are you crying?

LINDA: I was just . . . Yeah.

FRANK: What's wrong? Oh, my beautiful . . .

LINDA: Oh, Frank.

FRANK: What?

LINDA: Look at you, you're so good. There isn't a mean bone in your body.

FRANK: Sure there is. Sometimes . . . when the light is about to turn red . . . I'll make like I'm gonna pull out with my cart and . . . you know, I flip out the bicyclists—or I'll pretend I don't see them and sneak the edge of it out around a truck and I know it's gonna make them swerve . . . this one guy hit a cab and fractured his collar bone, and fuck, I'm like . . . sick of those bozos disobeying the traffic lights . . .

LINDA: You are the biggest . . . If you think that's . . . You are a goof. Drawn back from the precipice, I realized he was too shallow to . . . I mean, two voices in my head, one saying, Tell him your plan, love him, reveal everything, he's not a bad man, and the other one saying, Fry him, nail the motherfucker.

HUSH: That's—

LINDA: Yes, the Devil, that was the Devil, and I gave the Devil his due. Jump cut, five *years: (Another day, much later. Sings)* Happy birthday, dear Frannnnnk! Happy birthday to you! Make a wish, don't tell me. What did you wish?

FRANK: Well—

LINDA: Of course he told.

FRANK: I wished that we could grow old together and . . . I don't know, maybe open a vegetarian restaurant or something.

LINDA: Frank is not stronger than the drug. Frank is not stronger than baby aspirin. Are you feeling it yet? . . . Me, too. My wish?

FRANK: What?

LINDA: To quit that fucking store.

FRANK: Poof. Your wish is my command. Shazam!

(He presents a check.)

LINDA: Whoa.

FRANK: Right?

LINDA: Let's . . . I know . . . what I really want this second . . . or . . .

FRANK: What?

LINDA: To put it all out here on the floor in, I mean, lots of it, small bills, not too small, I don't know, and . . . make love on it, as like . . . a promise to the future.

(Pause.)

FRANK: Now?

LINDA: Like . . . whenever, I don't know . . . And damn if he
didn't go to the bank with three forms of identification
and take out one million dollars in large bills . . .

HUSH: They let you do that?

LINDA: Apparently. And—we hadn't even paid the tax on it
yet.

HUSH: This ain't true.

LINDA: We're tripping our brains out, or he thinks we are, he
is, I am stone cold sober . . . Okay . . .

(Later. Frank's got the cash.)

Oh, wait.

FRANK: What?

(She reveals a pair of handcuffs.)

LINDA: Want to chain me down?

FRANK: What?

LINDA: Do you?

FRANK: Do you . . . Is that what you want?

LINDA: Yes.

FRANK: How do I . . . ?

LINDA: Here, you just . . .

*(She attaches one of the handcuffs to him and the other end
to something solid; then produces a roll of masking tape,
wraps it around his mouth, all during:)*

And then you can like . . .

FRANK: You have the key.

LINDA: Here's the key. And then you could . . . You could
wrap it around me . . .

FRANK: Hey.

LINDA: I'm not gonna hurt you . . . Without a doubt, in the
entire world, I would say in the entire galaxy . . . there
is no creature more guileless than you . . . When you
try to find me . . . you will I hope learn at last that there

are in fact people out there who know what they want and mean to get it and do, all the time, at other people's expense, people who are perfectly willing to take and take and take and take . . . having listened to you come like a baboon, and weep and moan and scream every little eeny orgasm . . . none of our neighbors are going to react to your sounds for hours . . . and by then . . . Bye, honey. Don't let the bedbugs bite. Oh . . .

(She douses Frank with lighter fluid, then lights a match.)

I knew there was something. Angel, Devil, Angel, Devil. Should I? . . . Will I? Can I? Must I? Oh, honey, what do *you* want? Do you want me to throw this match on you? No?

(She moves it closer to him.)

I'm sorry, what was your answer? . . . Oh, no, that's right, you *don't* want me to light you. Is that right? *(Pause)* Okay.

(She keeps moving the match closer and closer.)

Okay . . . Okay . . . That's what you want . . . And *I* want . . .

(She extinguishes the match and leaves. Frank disappears.)

Have you ever seen those photos from Germany during the war? With the Jews in the streets being made to pray on their knees or having their beards sliced off: everyone is laughing; not just the soldiers, the people all along the sidewalk are laughing . . . any one of them could have picked up a little Jewish boy and bashed his brains out against a wall and gone home for supper with the kiddies . . . so . . . I understand that now. Power.

(The Stewardess comes by with a cart.)

A glass of cranberry juice, no ice, please.

STEWARDESS: For you?

HUSH: Water, please.

STEWARDESS: Water?

LINDA: Your turn.

HUSH: What happened to . . .

LINDA: Frank? No idea. Oh, I left one piece of critical information out: I wasn't beautiful: weak chin, thin lips, peculiar nose. So this is not the way I looked at the time. With money you can buy a new social security number, did you know that? And you can even change your height, make yourself shorter, if you don't like your height. They take a little length out of here and here, and reattach all the nerves and muscles and arteries, veins, sinew—*bone*. Alter the shape of your jaw, the color of your eyes . . . Life is a bounty of opportunity. So am I the Devil?

HUSH: You're making that up.

LINDA: Am I? . . . It's certainly possible. But . . . *(She shows him the inside of her bag)* You are the only being in the universe who knows where I am.

(Pause.)

HUSH: No.

LINDA: No? Oh, besides God. And Satan. The Trinity! And you don't know my real name, and I'm not staying in Seattle, I've rented a little cabin as far out in the woods as a person can go . . . no phone, not even my parents know where I'm going, we've lost touch with each other . . . so you will never find me or see me again which is why I feel comfortable telling you, my father confessor. *(Short pause)* My rage: dispensed. In one . . . It was fan. Tastic.

HUSH: Fear?

LINDA: No fear.

HUSH: No—Fear? Is just the absence of God.

LINDA: Oh.

HUSH: Fear and Hate. Are the absence of God. God is Love.

LINDA: Yes, I saw the film.

HUSH: You've let evil into your heart, as we all do, but Jesus Christ the Redeemer forgives you and wraps his arms around you. Declare your soul to him and you will never be afraid: to fly, to face the truth, his final judgment.

LINDA: You're very sweet . . . You are . . . What was your crime? What did you do?

HUSH: It doesn't matter.

LINDA: It does to me . . .

HUSH: Why do you think you're afraid to fly?

LINDA: White collar crime?

HUSH: Supposed to be the safest form of travel, isn't it?

LINDA: Thalidomide was supposed to be safe, nuclear power. I think I'm afraid to fly because of all that open space. I'm terrified of . . . too much.

HUSH: Mm-hm.

LINDA: It scares me what's going on in all those houses after dark, lit up—

HUSH: Yes.

LINDA: Like—

HUSH: Sin.

LINDA: You just know somebody's drinking too much and hiding, this is not aimed at you, but hiding behind their religion while they make their little kids . . . I like rooms with doors. I think too much choice is what's wrong with America. I do. You too? . . . But you've just been in . . . Murder? Rape? . . . No? Okay, don't tell me, let me guess.

HUSH: No.

LINDA: Ummm, assault? Drugs? Theft. Fifteen years. I give up. What else is there? . . .

HUSH: Most of the guys you meet in prison are there on drug charges.

LINDA: Are they? Well, it makes total sense . . . most of the country is on something, and believe me, it's not the heroin addicts sexually assaulting their kids, I've been to AA, okay? . . . Judges, preachers: all hiding behind, again, sorry, the Bible. While . . . Freud thought they were imagining it: that their brothers and uncles and neighbors and mothers and fathers were fucking them, raping babies, babies, but . . . the . . . nice thing about a child, is a child will do anything to accommodate its parents, because its parents are God . . . so they make it okay, somehow . . . it is . . . an ancient rite of passage . . . for the child to survive . . . the human animal . . . Concealed weapon? . . . Not white collar. You seem, I don't know, you don't seem uneducated to me. You seem perfectly sane.

HUSH: You think everyone in prison is uneducated or . . .

LINDA: Well . . .

HUSH: Crazy?

LINDA: Yeah, I do. More or less. Or greedy. Or, not insane, but . . . hurt, maltreated, beat up, or . . .

HUSH: Evil.

LINDA: Kidnapping! *(Pause)* Yes? . . . Oh . . . But not rape or murder? So . . . *(Pause)* Did you get a ransom? *(Pause)* Did you make some profit at least? . . . What?

HUSH: You're crazy.

LINDA: I am? No, what?, they caught you first.

HUSH: What is it, why do you want to know all this?

LINDA: You seem . . . I don't know, you seem at peace. I would . . . give a great deal to feel that . . .

HUSH: Accept Jesus into—

LINDA *(Overlapping "Jesus")*: I know, Jesus Christ in my heart . . .

HUSH: You can't say it, you have to feel it . . .

LINDA: I know . . .

HUSH: But do you . . . ?

LINDA: . . . I don't know. No. Maybe. *(Pause)* Was it your kid or your wife you kidnapped? Stranger? . . . Man or woman? . . .

HUSH: Girl.

LINDA: Little girl?

HUSH: Seventeen.

(Pause.)

LINDA: You kidnapped a little girl? . . . *(Pause)* Okay. Thanks for . . . sharing. I haven't been following—What is this movie? *(Pause)* Look, whatever, I'm proud of you for finding, for getting your . . . You seem self-possessed and solid and clear about your future, and I wish you nothing but well, whatever you did . . . Your God seems like a real one, a genuine . . . Savior, to you, so . . . And . . . I'll tell you one more thing: if I were just to meet you on a plane or anywhere . . . I think you're very . . . appealing, unless I knew what you just told me, I wouldn't be afraid of you at all or—I'm not saying I am afraid of you, not at all. The opposite.

(Chime.)

STEWARDESS *(Over speaker)*: Ladies and gentlemen, the captain has turned on the FASTEN SEAT BELT sign. We expect to encounter some turbulence.

LINDA: Great.

STEWARDESS *(Over speaker)*: You should now return to your seats and fasten your seat belts.

LINDA *(Overlapping)*: This, okay, this is not a come on at all, this is a story, something that— . . . Oh, I can't.

HUSH: What?

LINDA: I can't . . . Oh, you just told me . . . Do you know what the Mile High Club is? Oh. No, okay, it's . . . Watch, she's gonna turn around, she has to know. The Mile High Club is an unofficial club of people who all . . . Look, look! Who have all had sex on airplanes, it's common knowledge, anyway. See?, even that woman has heard of the Mile High Club, she's probably the president. I was in Denver, getting my surgery, and they did as much as they could all at once, because it's traumatic physically and psychically so . . . chin, lips, nose, ears, tucks, snips, leg slices, so I was a mess, and very anesthetized . . . and I did not know—

(Turbulence growing through the following:)

Oh. God. That Denver is known as the Mile High City, because of its altitude, it is.

HUSH: It's all right.

LINDA: Anyway, next to my neighbor's room was a plaque—

(Another bump, spilling Linda's cranberry juice.)

Jeez. They left me on the gurney for a second, zonked—I'm okay—and this bronze plaque said THIS ROOM HAS BEEN DONATED BY THE MILE HIGH KENNEL CLUB. And when the nun came to wheel me into my room post-op, I said to her very distinctly, because I was bothered by it: "Who would want to have sex with a dog in an airplane?" Well, she might.

(More violent turbulence.)

Ohhhh.

HUSH: It's okay.

LINDA: Tell me something, anything. Tell me a story. What's prison like? Who was your cellmate? *(To an unseen passenger)* Oh, turn around, I'm afraid, all right? . . . Get a life.

HUSH: Almighty God and Father of us all, we thank Thee—

LINDA: That's okay.

HUSH: —that with us Thy ways of love and mercy are known. Thou dost love us with an everlasting love and dost restore us again and again; yet we are prone toward unfaithfulness to Thee and vengefulness toward our fellow man—

LINDA: I'll say.

HUSH: —while Thou art ever merciful. Help us to love Thee as we ought [. . .] and fill us with compassion for each

other that we may be worthy of being called followers
of Thy compassionate Son, Jes—
HUSH AND LINDA: [Je]sus Christ—
HUSH: Our Lord.

(Linda repeats after him.)

HUSH AND LINDA: Let the power of Thy Spirit descend upon
us in this hour that, worshipping Thee in spirit and
truth, we may be saved from all coldness of heart and
inhospitality of spirit. Let Thy name be honored as we
lift up our hearts to Thee, and bless each expectant
worshipper with the light of Thy countenance: Jesus
Christ our Lord. Amen.
LINDA: Coldness of heart and . . .
HUSH: Inhospitality of spirit.
LINDA: Inhospitality of spirit.
HUSH: The greatest sin is that.
LINDA: Inhospitality? You're kidding.
HUSH: The sin of Sodom and Gomorrah.
LINDA: I thought that was . . . Hey, no turbulence. Thanks . . .
Inhospitality . . .
HUSH: Of spirit.

(Pause.)

LINDA: Uhhh. Thank you. *(Longer pause)* Thank you. *(Pause)*
Hospitality.

(Pause.)

HUSH: You know, you don't always have to be the same—so
afraid. *(Short pause)* When I was fifteen?
LINDA: Uh-huh?
HUSH: I heard voices telling me things . . . what to do, who
to listen to . . . I knew I wasn't supposed to tell anybody . . . that the voices were another world, speaking
. . . through me; I'd been selected, and I felt special . . .

They said I was God. They said I had created the world, it was, everything, everybody . . . all . . . everybody was pretending that I wasn't who I really was . . . and so I had to say the right things, do the right things . . .

LINDA: Uh-huh.

HUSH: Or . . . it would all explode . . . and everything would be destroyed, I could do that, the part of me that knew the truth . . . Their suffering would all have been useless. They were the voices of saints who'd suffered torment—

LINDA *(A nod, or a very quiet)*: Uh-huh.

HUSH: —fire, knives, arrows, all of them—singing— Even buying a pack of gum, it was important what coins I used, whether they were copper or silver, nickel plate . . . Everything had a symbolism. Which is how the Devil works, in symbols. God works through Love—Love alone. But I didn't know that. I thought it was God, I thought it was me talking to me . . . from deep outside and inside. Probably what . . . I don't know, probably what the pope thinks, that he speaks for God. Or the ayatollah. That's always the Devil, if you think you speak for God. But I didn't know that. And the voices got louder and, I started flunking out. My parents were really freaked. They were in denial. I was being bad. By the time they threw me out . . . I couldn't hold a reasonable conversation, I was possessed by the voices telling me: "Don't look this person in the eye, that is Satan, you are holding everything in balance, the stars, you are the universe itself." I was hospitalized, picked up by the cops and put in a state home, and medicated; they said the urges were me, mine, which I couldn't acknowledge, so I assigned them to "outside"—"others"—that I identified with the martyred saints, and it was my own anger projected onto imaginary— Anyway I was released. My hair fell out. I was living in an abandoned cottage in Coburn, you know where that is? Way out . . . Living off garbage and stolen cans. I would wander around in New Hope after dark, and panhandle. I had this old car. And the voices said . . .

to kill a girl. She had to be the right girl. I had to . . . fix myself up, cut my beard, buy a new shirt, cologne, and spruce up, go to a bar. And I would know who she was, God would tell me: she was to be the sacrifice, like the Inca, you know?, the ancient people? They would pick a virgin, a little girl, and dope her up, march her up the side of the mountain and bash her skull in. To appease the gods. And it was an honor. And I was the last true voice of the True God. She would join them: the hosts of all the saints, the angels. *(Pause)* Her name was Diane, she was tall, had dark hair, kind of funny features, kinda like an Inca girl, I think . . . And I chatted her up. I could hold it together if I knew there was a reason, a purpose, and I invited her back to my cabin and she came . . . We drove, it's a long long way, and she seemed excited, and not afraid. And we got there, I didn't have electricity, just lamps, and an oil burner, all hippie-like, I told her it was an ethical choice, I wasn't stupid. I'm not stupid.

LINDA: No.

HUSH: Told her I had to go pee, and when I came out of the bathroom, I . . . and kissed her, and . . . I chained her up. And a voice in me was saying, "Don't do it, don't do it." And I thought that was the Devil. But I couldn't . . . I couldn't be sure . . . And the voice of God, the voices I thought was God said, "Kill her quick. With your teeth, anything." But they were in battle . . . Join her . . . to us, join her to Sebastian and Joan and Saint Catherine . . . The two . . . And so . . . I thought I'd keep her alive until I could know, for sure, and I . . . put her in a trunk. And kept her there.

LINDA: For how long?

HUSH: I fed her and let her wash and go to the bathroom.

LINDA: How long?

HUSH: Long time.

LINDA: How long?

HUSH: Long, while I . . . fought it out. God and the Devil. I had 'em confused.

LINDA: Are you on medication now? Good. Don't stop taking it. It's, obviously it's working. Some people stop and . . .

HUSH: I found the True God. I don't really need it.

LINDA: Yes, you do. Trust me. I know a lot about this. It doesn't even work for some people, a lot of people, so you're lucky. I'm glad you found God, but don't stop the medication, all right? . . . How long was she in the trunk?

(Pause.)

HUSH: A year.

(Silence.)

LINDA: A year? The voices in your head told you to keep . . . a stranger— You didn't know her . . . For a year? Locked up? . . .

HUSH: I had her in chains.

LINDA: Uh-huh. *Oh*, well, the voices in your head told you to . . . keep a complete stranger in a trunk . . . for a year? In chains. Well . . . The Devil made you do it. *(Pause)* What would you say to her . . . if . . . ? Imagine I'm that woman, what would you say to her now?

HUSH: I'm sorry. All I can . . .

LINDA: Oh. I'm sorry. Whoops. My mistake. Voices, how convenient.

(Pause.)

HUSH: You tortured your friend, you doused him, waved a match—

LINDA: Yes. Oh, that's the same. I didn't do it for a *year*! I knew him, he was . . . I'm gonna look for another seat, that is . . . *(Pause)* No, you're right, I'm sorry . . . I'm sorry . . . but . . . when you said you knew the Devil, you meant you knew the Devil. That is . . . *(Pause)* Why didn't you just kill her, wouldn't that have been more merciful? For a year she thought she was going to be ... What, did her family come after you?, and find her? No? What kind of ... ? I'm sorry, I'm just trying to wrap my mind around ... Do you think Hitler heard voices? Maybe? ... You were abused, weren't you? How old?

HUSH: Let he who is without sin cast the first stone.

LINDA: Uh-huh. That's really obnoxious. Turn the other cheek while I ... stick it up inside you, up your ass, is that what happened? Did you bleed?

HUSH: It's not for man to judge. I fill my heart with Christ's forgiveness, I shine—

LINDA: Oh, stop it! What is wrong with you? How can you ... I'm just ... You scared me. I would have gone home with you, I would, in an instant ... that could've been *me*. Do you understand? *(Pause)* You've found ... your peace somehow. Your, you've found great peace. Despite everything; despite what you've done.

HUSH: Nothing I can do can ev[er]—

LINDA: Nothing can change it, I know. I wish, honest to God, your God, not just any God, that I had that kind of peace.

(Pause.)

HUSH: You can.

LINDA: I did, I tortured him. You're right. For ... some ... several minutes, I think, I ... enjoyed torturing him, getting back at him, my father, my mother, the world ... some part of me ...

HUSH: It is in your power—

LINDA: The power. Over his life. I ... I enjoyed that. The way ... some men talk about hunting, the right to bear arms ... the right to do harm. To hurt ... I know that ...

(Pause.)

HUSH: You can choose another way.

LINDA: Oh, please.

HUSH: You can.

(Pause.)

LINDA: Help me.

HUSH: You don't need me.

LINDA: Will you help me? I trust you. I don't know why.
But . . . I do. *(Pause)* You said you wanted to help people, help me. Please? Let me see what you take, may I?

HUSH: You shouldn't take it.

LINDA: No, no, I just want to see . . .

(He shows her his medication.)

My cousin was schizophrenic and they put him on
this, this very drug, and he turned into a vegetable
practically. So you're lucky. God has smiled on you,
you know. You should share that. With anybody and
everybody who asks. He stopped taking the drug and
disappeared, and no one knows if he's alive or dead . . .

HUSH: I'm sorry.

LINDA: . . . Would you do me a favor? . . .

HUSH: If I can.

LINDA: Promise me?

HUSH: If . . .

LINDA: I know what I've done is wrong, I know I've sinned.
I know that's why I'm afraid.

HUSH: Invite God in.

LINDA: I want to die. I want to kill myself . . .

HUSH: No.

LINDA: Yes. I do.

HUSH: You feel that way now. When Jesus comes into your
life, you feel like a child again.

LINDA: Show me.

HUSH: Just say it, Lord Almighty God . . .

LINDA: Come—I can't here— Come stay with me at my cabin?

HUSH: No.

LINDA: I want to believe, but I don't.

HUSH: Say the words, invite him in.

LINDA: I'm gonna take an overdose, I'm afraid I'm going to kill myself.

HUSH: Jesus Christ, My Immortal Savior—

LINDA: I won't touch you, I have two beds . . . See? *(She shows him her pills)* Please. Help me, if you're gonna help someone. I can't live.

HUSH: Yes, you can, say the words with me.

LINDA: Please, Hush, teach me what you know.

HUSH: Jesus Christ—

LINDA: For one night. Please. Call your friend you're staying with, say you've found a place for one night, I'm lost . . . I know I need— *(To an unseen passenger)* Oh, turn around!, not everything in life is for your entertainment . . . I know I need God. I'm afraid. *(Pause)* Oh, it's all right. You don't . . . I'm not your responsibility . . . I understand.

HUSH: All right.

LINDA: You will? Thank you. I won't abuse the privilege, just this one night, I promise . . . Thank you. Oh, I feel . . . A total stranger. You're something . . . I feel light . . . I . . . sometimes I want to die.

HUSH: I know.

LINDA: Is that God? . . . the lightness? Light as . . . light as *light!* Thank you . . . I'm exhausted . . . God . . .

CAPTAIN *(Over speaker)*: Ladies and gentlemen, we will soon be beginning our descent into the Sea-Tac airport. If you need to leave your seat for any reason, we suggest you do so now before I turn on the seat belt sign for the final leg of our journey . . . We know you have a choice of airlines and so I want to take this opportunity to thank you for flying with us tonight . . .

A cabin in the woods. Hush lights a gas lamp; he is younger. With him is Diane. She speaks with a North Carolina accent.

DIANE: Cool. Wow.

HUSH: You like something to drink?

DIANE: Sure. What do you have?

HUSH: I have some beer.

DIANE: Beer's fine.

HUSH: You were drinking, what was it?

DIANE: Lillet?

HUSH: Don't have any of that.

DIANE: That's all right. Honestly? Any beer is fine.

HUSH: So your family . . . ?

DIANE: You have a really intense energy, you know that? When you were at the bar, even with your back to me, I could feel . . . some people just have . . . something . . . crackling, like a power station. You do. In spades! Heat, electricity, magnetism, ego. Honestly.

(Pause.)

HUSH: You, too.

DIANE: Thanks. Yeah, my family. Ummmm, they're kind of a titular family, if you know what I mean . . . Family only nominally speaking . . . In appearance only, I mean, yeah. I left home at fifteen and haven't seen them, only spoke to my mom a couple of times.

HUSH: Really?

DIANE: Yeah. Annnd, this is pretty, your place, it's wild . . . Good place to write.

HUSH: Go on.

DIANE: Uhhhh, that's what I love about strangers . . . If you sit in a coffee shop and watch people walk by or listen in to their conversations at the other table, or meet somebody . . . like this . . . No history, all fresh clean blank slate . . . chance . . . promise,—

HUSH: Uh-huh.

DIANE: —possibility. I love that. Mystery. Danger. Romance. *(Pause)* It's neat.

HUSH: It is.

DIANE: Honestly? First thing, when I looked at you, I thought . . . Wait a minute, there's something—What? *(Pause)* Are you hearing something? . . . What?

HUSH: That . . . There . . . little . . . in there—

DIANE: Oh, yeah.

HUSH: I gotta tighten that.

DIANE: You do your own plumbing?

HUSH: Well, sure.

DIANE: Of course.

HUSH: Who else is gonna—

DIANE: You would. Back to . . . back to nature. So what's your book about?

HUSH: Oh, it's not good . . .

DIANE: Oh? I—

HUSH: . . . to give too much away before . . . you . . .

DIANE: The creative process.

HUSH: Yeah, so . . .

DIANE: Is it your first novel?

HUSH: Maybe this wasn't such a good idea, you know.

DIANE: What? . . . You mean . . .

HUSH: My stomach.

DIANE: Oh, are you not feeling well?

HUSH: Maybe . . . It's o— . . . It's okay.

DIANE: Well, I can't . . . You'd have to drive, I can't walk all the way back to New Hope, it's, how long is it?

HUSH: It's okay. I . . . That *noise.*

DIANE: I . . . I barely hear it, honestly.

HUSH: Why do you keep saying that? "Honestly." "Honestly."

(Pause.)

DIANE: Yeah, you should drive me back. I'm sorry.

HUSH: It's okay. I've got to take a whizz.

DIANE: Sure. Then . . .

(Hush goes into the bathroom. Pause. Finally he emerges.)

HUSH: Sorry. I'm—

DIANE: It's okay.

HUSH: I wrote and wrote and wrote, two days straight, I haven't slept.

DIANE: I understand.

HUSH: Sorry.

DIANE: It's okay.

HUSH: You're very pretty.

DIANE: Well. *(Pause)* Thank you. *(Pause)* You . . . We should go.

HUSH: Yes. Sorry.

DIANE: It's fine.

HUSH: . . . I shouldn't . . .

DIANE: It's really okay.

(Pause.)

HUSH: Okay.

DIANE: Some other time.

HUSH: Some other time.

DIANE: Let's—

HUSH: May I . . . kiss you?

DIANE: Oh. I don't, yes, sure . . .

HUSH: Is it . . . ?

DIANE: Okay.

(Pause. They kiss.)

Mmmm. Mmmmm. I feel . . . What's that? You're trying to . . . change my mind. Unh-uhn.

HUSH: No, I'm not. Let's go.

DIANE: Okay. *(Pause)* Okay.

HUSH: What?

DIANE: You're just a little boy, aren't you? . . . Okay.

HUSH: Go ahead.

*(She starts toward the door but he overpowers her, hand-
cuffing her wrist to her ankle; as they struggle:)*

DIANE: What are you doing? Get off! No. Please. Please, oh
please don't do this. Hush, don't, I'm your friend—I
swear, I won't tell anyone, let me go, please—Help!
Please don't please don't hurt me, please, don't hurt
me. Goddamn you—help! Help! Help me. Somebody
help!

*(He has at last wrestled her into a trunk, and shut her
inside. Long pause.*

*Dissolve back into the present: Linda's cabin. She is
making tea for Hush and herself.)*

LINDA: Was there any part of it that was . . . thrilling? That—

HUSH: Yes.

LINDA: There was. Thank you. I want to understand. How
you got from one place . . . The place I understand . . .
where their eyes are pleading and your own heart is
pounding . . . where their life is in your hands . . .

HUSH: I could do anything, she belonged to me.

LINDA: Yes. He belonged to me. His existence. He was . . .

HUSH: Yeah.

LINDA: An object.

HUSH: A thing.

(Pause.)

LINDA: We're alike . . . in . . . the first half of our stories . . .
but . . . how do you acquit yourself?

(She brings him his tea.)

HUSH: Thanks.

LINDA: Forgive yourself, I mean. It's herbal.

HUSH: Christ.

LINDA: I hope that's okay.

HUSH: Christ does. Christ takes care of all of it.

LINDA: It has no caffeine, it'll help you sleep. *(Pause)* This . . .
I don't know, this might . . . I mean, I didn't—I had
nothing against Frank, he pissed me off sometimes,
but . . . you couldn't hate Frank, there was nothing to
hate, there wasn't—I liked him . . . I, I mean, did you
like her? . . . The girl? D'you talk to each other? You
must've. *(Pause)* In all that time? . . . *(Pause)* Did you
hate her? . . .

HUSH: Why am I here?

LINDA: I . . . Whhh—?

HUSH: Where's the other bed?

LINDA: Oh.

HUSH: You said there were—

LINDA: Up in the attic, you can help me bring it down, it's a
cot . . . I forgot I put it up there, you want to get it
now? We can. *(Pause)* You're . . . I hope . . . you're here
to help me. Aren't you? *(Pause)* You said you wanted to
help people. The way you'd been helped. Find . . .
Didn't you? . . . All I want is to understand.

HUSH: Understanding is the booby prize. The peace that pas-
seth all understanding. You ever hear that? *(Pause)* Hey.

LINDA: Hey.

HUSH: Give me the pills. The ones you were going to take.

LINDA: Oh.

HUSH: I don't want you swallowing them after I go to sleep which could make me an accessory to a crime.

LINDA *(Giving him her pills)*: I guess it's something you have to think about. I can't even imagine. *(Short pause)* Why'd you pick her? I mean, I know, the voices, but . . . what was it about her? *(Pause)* If this is too difficult. Did you feel sorry for her? Did you think she deserved to die?

HUSH: That isn't the way it was.

LINDA: Well . . . was she the kind of woman, I mean, would you have dated her? In other . . . What?

HUSH: Date. [It]'s such a funny word.

LINDA: Why? *(Pause)* Didn't you ever date people?

HUSH: By the time I was in high school, I barely spoke—

LINDA: Uh-huh.

HUSH: —to people; I wouldn't let them near me, I'd say as little as possible and move away.

LINDA: What about . . . earlier? *(Pause)* You've always been alone.

HUSH: . . . Earlier's the place I never go.

LINDA . . . Why?

HUSH: [It]'s too good. [It]'s like another life. Somebody else's.

LINDA: Then . . . I would think you'd like to remember that . . . Wouldn't you?

HUSH: Why? So I could remind myself I can't have it?

LINDA: Why can't you have it? . . . Can't you try again?

HUSH: Try what? Be eight again? Be tucked in, be told things, and believe; be kissed; I'm not feeling sorry for myself, I'm being honest. I won't be. I won't believe. I won't be kissed.

LINDA: Why?

(Pause.)

HUSH: I'm trying to tell you. *(Silence)* I want to strike out, I have urges.

LINDA: People want to do things all the time—steal things, kill people, burn . . . buildings. That's . . . It's human. That doesn't mean they . . . are compelled. There's a difference between feelings and actions.

HUSH: Then you don't have to kill yourself.

LINDA: And you don't have to strike out.

(Pause.)

HUSH: You don't understand.

LINDA: No.

HUSH: All the things . . . If I think, and I don't, I promise you, when these thoughts come up, I let them go: I refuse to follow them back to . . .

(Pause.)

LINDA: Where?

HUSH: Oh . . . washing the car with my dad, tickled, being tickled by my sister, you're trying to trick me, aren't you? School, haircuts, school projects . . . A book on transportation: all cutout pictures from magazines and pasted on construction paper? That was a kind of . . . bliss—I start to look back on that, and . . .

LINDA: What?

HUSH: Rips my heart out of my chest. My family'd . . . they have injunctions out against me, they'd never take me back. Burying me is easier than looking at me.

LINDA: Make your own family.

(Pause.)

HUSH: Yeah. I can't even see myself in a picture with other people . . . without destroying them.

(Pause.)

LINDA: That's why you have to save them. *(Pause)* That's just a fear. *(Pause)* Did anybody ever come around after you'd . . . ? I mean, checking on you or hear, what was her name?

HUSH: Diane.

LINDA: Scream?

HUSH: . . . She stopped after a few days.

LINDA: Screaming? . . . What was that like? . . . listening to that?

(From inside the trunk we begin to hear muffled screams.)

HUSH: Like a gnawing, an agony . . . sort of like when a little baby screams and screams and nothing you can do will stop it, you want to hit it finally, shut it up. I liked it, too, because it was my "God" saying, "Kill her, go ahead, put her out of this pain, do it now. Now! Hurry up . . . Save the universe. Save mankind. Join her to *us.*" *(Pause)* Finally, she stopped. *(Silence)* . . . I'd come home from . . . looking for food . . . panhandling. She hardly ever spoke to me after those first few days. Nothing for a long time. What?

LINDA: I was going to make a joke. In bad taste. "Some women are just so touchy. Put 'em in a trunk and they freeze you out." You're right . . . Bad Devil! Down. Go on. Sorry.

HUSH: You're nuts.

LINDA: Oh, the kettle speaks about the other kitchen appliances. *I'm* nuts. So, I'm Satan, I can't help it, I'm trying to work on myself, cut me some slack. I'm in therapy!

HUSH: You make jokes about everything.

LINDA: That's how I survive. I'll try not to make so many jokes, all right, that's the best I can do is try. *(Short pause)* I'll *try.*

(Hush places a chair in the middle of the room.)

HUSH: Try to move that chair.

LINDA: What?

HUSH: Try to move this chair. *(Pause)* Try.

LINDA: Move it where?

HUSH: Anywhere. Try to move it an inch.

LINDA: Are you . . . ? What, are you hyperkinetic or something? You can control objects? *(She pretends she can't
budge the chair)* No, I can't move it. Oh my god! You *are*
Satan!

(She moves the chair.)

HUSH: Uhn-uhn. I said try. You moved it. I said, "*Try* to
move it."

LINDA: Oh, I see. What [did I say] . . . ?

HUSH: You said you were gonna try to stop making jokes.

LINDA: Ah, yes.

HUSH: That's like trying to quit smoking. Anybody tells you
they're trying to quit ain't gonna do it. Doing and trying to do are two different things. One's a lie. It's like
when your parents say, "Maybe." It's a lie, means no. If
you're gonna try to stop doing something, you're not
gonna stop. If you're doing something, you're not trying, you're doing it. You either accept Jesus or you
don't, it's no more complicated than that.

LINDA: Just . . . say the words.

HUSH: No, that's like trying. Just mean the words.

LINDA: Mean the words. I accept Jesus into my heart. I accept
Jesus into my heart.

HUSH: There you go.

LINDA: I, Linda Asnitz, accept Jesus into my heart. I invite
him in, I accept him, I . . . embrace—

HUSH: That's enough, it'll do. *(Pause)* How do you feel?

(A shrug. Pause.)

LINDA: I still want to know how you fought for a year,
against . . . People usually do something or they don't,

isn't that what you were just saying? They don't try not to do it, I agree with you.

(Pause.)

HUSH: You didn't kill . . .

LINDA: Frank?

HUSH: Frank.

LINDA: I didn't want to, I wanted to humiliate him. If I'd wanted to kill him, I could have gotten away with it. Otherwise . . . You must have wanted something else from her. Diane.

HUSH: Like?

LINDA: You tell me. *(Silence)* What stopped you? . . . What were your voices saying?, what did you hear? Exactly. Can you tell me?

(Hush rises, unlocks the trunk, lifts the lid as we return to the past.

Diane stands—filthy, her clothes have not been cleaned, her hair is stringy, unwashed; she is chained to the trunk by one ankle. Hush turns his back to her, speaks to her:)

HUSH: There's some food on the counter. I saw 'em leave it on the table, it wasn't in the trash or sitting around for long. 'S'the best I can do.

(Hush sits. As Diane eats, Hush does the voices inside his head.)

"She'll struggle and kick. Her eyes'll beg. Popping out of her head. You'll be God, you'll be God, you'll be God. Merciless, merciful, mercy . . . Power, electric power, electrocution, suffocation, manpower, slicing open her windpipe, air power, air breath, air death, no breath, no, evil." Like that, on and on and on, even in sleep. No rest from—

(Diane shuffles over toward Hush who takes out a knife and points it toward her, tries not to look her in the eye.)

"Not the eye, not the eye, eye power, eye sockets electric dead-eye-dick-dead—"

(Diane shows Hush a sore on her ankle.)

How'd you do that? . . . "Let her go, no, cut her leg off."

DIANE: Move the chain.

HUSH: . . . Sorry, can't do that. "Cut. Saint."

DIANE: It's gonna get infected and then I'm gonna die and then you'll be guilty of murder—

HUSH: "Dead."

DIANE: —not just kidnapping.

HUSH: "Dead kid, dead kid."

(Pause.)

DIANE: This is not a relationship. If you think we're having a relationship, then you've never had one. I'm sorry. You let me go . . . someone will help you. You kill me or I die . . . I understand you. I see right through.

HUSH: "Done deed."

DIANE: Your heart I see . . . thinking we're having . . . thinking this is *something*. Your head. You'd have to do a whole lot more than bring home scraps and keep me locked up. And I'm not talking about sex, okay? I'm talking about showing . . . I'm talking about you . . . There's some good part of you, I see it. There. You can't keep all that shit locked away and eating at you, that's like maggots, and you're gonna fall apart like an old piece of meat. *(Pause)* So you can kill me. But then your love affair is over, and it's on to the next . . . It's not so fun to talk to me when I'm cold and rotting and getting all leathery.

(Pause.)

HUSH: I'mmmm gonna have to chain it to your other ankle, so you walk more careful, don't pull on it. *(Silence)* "Okay, do it, okay, do it."

(Hush unlocks the cuff on her wounded ankle, never looking her in the eye.)

"No eye, no eyes, dead eyes—"

(Diane suddenly kicks Hush in the groin and strangles him with the chain. She seizes a heavy object and smashes it into his face, then runs out of the cabin.
Pause.)

LINDA: In . . . right in your face?

(He rises, unhurt.
It is the present once more.)

HUSH: Oh, yeah. Couldn't see out of this eye for a coupla weeks.
LINDA: . . . What did you do?
HUSH: Put ice on it.
LINDA: No, did—you go after her?
HUSH: By the time I came to . . . *(Pause)* I was relieved. Like the voice . . . It was quiet. I wanted to be caught.
LINDA: You did.
HUSH: Before it started. Again. I wanted the universe to collapse, I wanted the world to end. I wanted to face my God and say, "I have failed, I'm sorry." I wanted the war to be over.
LINDA: You were relieved. And she went to the police? . . . She— . . . *(Pause)* No? What happened?
HUSH: I sat and prayed . . .
LINDA: You prayed, what did you pray for?
HUSH: Quiet. *(Pause)* Just . . . quiet.
LINDA: And . . . ? *(Pause)* What happened?

HUSH: . . . And . . . eventually . . . I don't know, hours, minutes, I was so out of it . . . Eventually . . .

(Now we are in the present and the past together as Diane hobbles back in, her hair and clothing covered with burrs; new cuts, a wide scrape on her thigh, clothing torn.

With complete resignation, never looking at Hush, she crosses to the trunk, opens it and climbs back in.)

LINDA: She came . . . ?

HUSH: She was really bad this time.

LINDA: I don't understand.

HUSH: Cut up, bruised . . . She'd fallen and hit her head. She . . . crawled back into the trunk. I guess she'd only gotten so far . . . and realized how isolated we were and . . . it was fall, she was . . . probably afraid, it wasn't cold, not near. But . . .

LINDA: But—?

HUSH: But maybe she was afraid she would freeze . . . At night. But it was like sixty, though, that's the thing. She wouldn't. *(Pause)* She, actually, there was a ranger's station a couple of miles on the opposite side of us . . . I guess the first few times he looked in, he saw what a mess the place was and thought, Let the poor guy be warm at night, or something. Who else is gonna use it? He must have been so quiet she didn't hear him . . . Only she had a cold the last time he came and her cough . . . What's the matter?

(Pause.)

LINDA: She came . . . ?

HUSH: Back.

LINDA: . . . home.

HUSH: Yeah. After I was incarcerate—*home*, yeah—I saw an article in a newspaper. She said she'd missed . . . even after I was put away, she sometimes . . . missed . . . the—

HUSH AND LINDA: —trunk.

(Pause.)

HUSH: Yeah. So . . .

(He brings Diane a glass of something to drink, then gently wipes her wounds with a wet cloth—a strangely tender, isolated moment between the two.)

LINDA: What?
HUSH: So . . . I don't know.
LINDA: . . . What were you going to—?
HUSH: Maybe . . . I don't know.
LINDA: So maybe—?
HUSH: I don't know.
LINDA: You were . . . ?
HUSH: It was the Devil.
LINDA: Then say it.
HUSH: No.
LINDA: Help me.
HUSH: I cast him out.
LINDA *(Simultaneously)*: Please. I want to understand.
HUSH: I nursed her back to health.
LINDA: You were going to say, "So maybe *she*—"?
HUSH: I don't know.
LINDA: Yes.
HUSH: I kept her cuts from getting infected.
LINDA: Why would she—?
HUSH: I made sure she didn't have anything in the trunk to hurt herself with . . .
LINDA: Then why would she—
HUSH: *I don't know.*

(Pause.)

LINDA: Maybe she felt sorry for you.

HUSH: I didn't kill her! . . . I fed her with the best food I could find . . .

(Pause.)

LINDA: You made love to her.
HUSH: No. *He* wanted me to.
LINDA: Bullshit. I'm me now, even if there's Satan tempting me—
HUSH: I put everything—
LINDA *(Over, continuous)*: —bringing you here like this.
HUSH: —everything in God's hands.
LINDA: Maybe she knew you were more afraid than she was.
HUSH: Put your life in his hands.
LINDA: I've put my life in your hands, Hush. So—
HUSH: You shouldn't.
LINDA: That's as may be.

(They stare at each other in silence.)

Let's get the cot down, I'm tired.

(She opens a trap in the ceiling.)

HUSH: What were you doing in Philadelphia?
LINDA: Why?
HUSH: Why were you there?
LINDA: It isn't, oh, it isn't something I'm proud of. I'll tell you. I already confessed to Frank and the match and the lighter fluid. I'm afraid of heights if you didn't already notice. Would you mind handing it down?
HUSH: Tell me. Linda: I will. Can we . . . do this and talk?

(Hold. She leans in and kisses him on the cheek.)

I was in Philadelphia . . .

(Another kiss—gently on the lips.)

Wait, I'll get you a flashlight.

(Pause. He starts up the ladder.)

It should be up to the right, probably with all the old blankets. I'm just looking for a light, hold on.
HUSH: I don't see it.
LINDA: Move some of that stuff out of the way, can you?
HUSH: Yeah.

(Linda grabs the end of a chain which has been hidden; it is firmly attached to something immovable; on the other end is an open handcuff which she attaches to Hush's ankle.)

What are you . . . ? What . . . ? *(He lunges for her, but is caught up short. Painfully)* Help! Help!

(She takes out an enormous knife and sticks it into the cutting board.)

LINDA *(North Carolina accent, which she soon drops)*: Now you wish you'd killed me?
HUSH: The Lord is my shepherd, I shall not want. He restoreth my soul; He leadeth me—Yea, though I walk through the valley of the shadow of death, I will fear no evil: for Thou art with me; Thy rod and Thy staff they comfort me. Surely goodness and mercy shall follow me all the days of my life: and I will dwell in the house of the Lord forever. Amen.

(Silence.)

LINDA: Some people don't recover. Some people just. Won't. Get over it. For them God is an abstraction . . . even if they study the Bible.
HUSH: I'm sorry.

LINDA: Because they can't go anywhere, do anything, without feeling naked and insane. Some people are permanently raped.

HUSH: I did not.

LINDA: Soul, mind, peace, sanity . . . all raped . . . Finished.

HUSH: I'm sorry.

LINDA *(Quoting from the Bible)*: "When a stranger resides with you in your land, you shall not wrong him. The stranger who resides with you shall be to you as one of your citizens. You shall love him as yourself . . ."

(New day or night.)

HUSH: I have to go to the bathroom. *(Long pause)* I have to go. *(Pause)* I can't wait any longer.

(Pause. He soils himself. He quietly weeps.)

I'm going to need my pills.

(Linda finds his bottle of pills and moves into the toilet, all the while reciting:)

LINDA: "And the Lord spake unto Moses, saying: If a soul sin and commit a trespass [. . .] and lie unto his neighbor in that which was delivered him to keep, or in fellowship, or in a thing taken away by violence, or hath deceived his neighbor . . ."

*(Flush.
    Linda reenters.)*

HUSH: Please don't, I need them, please . . .

LINDA *(Over)*: ". . . in *any* of all these that a man doeth, sinning therein: then it shall be, because he hath sinned and is guilty, that he shall . . . *restore* . . . *that* . . . which he took violently away . . ."

HUSH: I can't. I can't restore . . . anything . . . only . . . you and God . . .

LINDA: ". . . He shall restore it in the principal, and shall add the fifth part more thereto, and give it . . . unto him—"

HUSH: Help! Help!

LINDA: "—to whom it appertaineth." God says you have to give everything back. And he says something else about . . . sacrificing a ram at the priests' . . . *(Pause)* "There can be no blemish on the ram."

(Later. Linda is in the kitchen.)

HUSH: You don't want to do this. I'm going to starve.

LINDA: You're going to tell me why.

HUSH: I told you.

LINDA: No. You can convince the parole board you've found God, and that's all you'll ever need . . .

(She tosses some food within Hush's reach; he eats.)

. . . And you can convince the doctors and maybe it's true . . . you hear voices . . . But if you do, then it isn't God who silenced them . . . And I will show you that . . .

HUSH: Tell you why . . . ?

LINDA: You didn't kill me.

HUSH: I didn't kill you because it was wrong.

LINDA: As opposed to keeping me in a trunk.

HUSH: It was the most wrong.

LINDA: Your God is too convenient, He forgives too much . . . *(Pause) Why? . . .*

(Silence.

Later. Linda sleeps; Hush is more agitated; he spots something just out of reach; with supreme effort he pulls against the chain, begins to edge it toward him with his toe.)

Have you tried stopping the drugs to see what would happen?

(She rises, moves the object out of his reach.)

HUSH: No. *Please.*

LINDA: So you don't really know if Jesus saves or Haldol saves . . . You're not afraid of the Devil, you're afraid of you.

HUSH *(Hearing voices)*: Pato . . .

LINDA: Aren't you?

HUSH: Pato.

LINDA: What? . . .

HUSH: My cellmate. Pato.

LINDA: What is he saying?

PATO'S VOICE: You have to choose.

LINDA: What?

HUSH: You choose.

LINDA: Choose.

HUSH AND PATO'S VOICE: You have to choose.

(Pato appears near Hush. Hush is now completely in the past, sharing a jail cell with Pato.)

PATO: The Lord doesn't give you anything you can't handle. *(Pause)* He doesn't.

LINDA: Tell me.

PATO: You should see the psychiatrist, you're hearing shit, I can see that, plain as day—in your head. What are they telling you? Kill people, right?

LINDA: What?

HUSH: Not people.

LINDA: Please.

HUSH: You, if you don't shut up.

PATO: There are no accidents, man. *(Pause)* There aren't.

LINDA: Can you hear me?

PATO: Christ brings us together for a reason.

HUSH: Then Christ must want me to pull the tongue out of your fucking mouth, don't think I won't. You heard what I did to get in here, didn't you?

(Pause.)

PATO: I'm not afraid. *(Silence)* A man may—
HUSH: *Hey!*
PATO: A man may kill me but he cannot harm me.
HUSH: I said shut up!
LINDA: Hush?
HUSH *(Over her)*: *Now!*

(Hush stands over Pato, arm poised to strike. Pause.)

PATO: Jesus sees—

(Hush hits him in the face, hard.)

God forgives all.

(Hush hits him again, again.)

God's love is—
HUSH: *Motherfuck!*
PATO: —all embracing. Turn the other cheek, he says.
HUSH: I'll turn your fucking cheek, you Chatty fucking Cathy! Get outa my head, understand? Hey, I want another cell, get me outa here, I want another cellmate! Hey!

(Silence. Hush sees Linda and returns to the present. Pato fades from view.)

LINDA: Now will you tell me? *(Pause)* Your parole officer told me all about your glorious conversion.
HUSH: Of course I'm filled with doubts! Of course I'm afraid. I'm not inhuman.
LINDA: I think that's debatable.
HUSH: I don't want to go back.
LINDA: To jail? To me?
HUSH: That man is a stranger.
LINDA: Why didn't you kill me?

HUSH: I don't know!
LINDA: Yes, you do, why!?!?

(Pause.)

HUSH: I liked it. I was excited.
LINDA: It?
HUSH: I enjoyed it.
LINDA: You didn't seem crazy, Hush.
HUSH: I liked that time.
LINDA: Yes . . . Just that? The time?
HUSH: I could taste it. It made me hard.
LINDA: It?
HUSH: Your fear.
LINDA: Me, you mean.
HUSH: Being quiet . . . in a room . . . with another human being.
LINDA: Me.
HUSH: Just being.
LINDA: Me.
HUSH: I loved it.
LINDA: Me.
HUSH: No!
LINDA: Yes!
HUSH: Pato! Save me!

(Again from the darkness; these lines overlap slightly:)

PATO'S VOICE *(Ricocheting right off of Hush's "Pato!")*: You choose.
HUSH: Save me.
LINDA: You still, Hush, you still want me!
HUSH *(Over her, to himself)*: Choose, you choose.

(Hush covers his ears and is once again in the jail cell with Pato, whose face is now swollen, bloody, cut, bruised. The "You!"s coming from all three create a cacophony inside Hush's head. His schizophrenia is in full flourish.)

PATO: You.

HUSH *(Meaning himself)*: You.

LINDA *(Overlapping)*: You hear me—

HUSH: You choose.

LINDA *(Continuous, not stopping)*: —and you know it's true!

PATO: You're choosing to live outside Christ's love.

LINDA: I have all the time in the world.

PATO: Just like you're choosing to live with those voices.

LINDA: You think after all I've done I can't wait?

PATO: If you can't shut 'em up yourself, go the infirmary and tell them what you hear and how many years you've heard it.

LINDA: I'm taking a shower.

(She exits into the bathroom; water is heard.)

PATO: Go ahead and cry.

HUSH: I'm not crying, just shut up. Jesus Christ!

PATO: Even in curses we call his name. *(Pause)* You know why I'm here? . . . I killed a little boy. In a hotel. A four-year-old boy. I heard him outside my door, in the hall. He was with his father on a trip, and when I heard his father say, "Stay by the door, I'm just going to get a newspaper," I opened the door and dragged him into the room. His father came running right away, but I had what I wanted: a little boy . . . I had what I wanted. And then it was over. They came finally and opened the door, but . . . Nothing ever mattered, I'd gotten what I needed, right? *(Silence)* We invite him in: Satan. You invited the Devil in . . . when you were too young to know what you were doing.

HUSH: I didn't make myself—[crazy], I heard the voices from the time I was twelve, I was *made*, God made me—

PATO: No.

PATO: —that way.

FRANK: Uhn-un. Satan. Saw your weakness, how hurt you were, how angry and helpless, and he gave you a sickness, planted there like a seed, but in *your hatred.* The voice that makes you a stranger unto yourself: that's him. He uses us. Inhabits us: finds the chink in the armor.

HUSH: Okay.

PATO: Whatever it is, and there's no way to fight, we just aren't strong enough. Only Jesus can take that weight.

(Linda comes out of the shower with little or no clothes—a towel; she dries herself.)

Only Jesus can take that weight. Only God can fight for us.

(Linda walks in front of Hush so that he can't help but see her.)

Unto death.

(Hush sees Linda, nearly naked; the word "death" reverberates; he is in the past and the present.)

It isn't any of us the Devil cares about, it's God.

HUSH: God.

PATO: He wants to get back at God.

(Linda moves slowly closer and closer to Hush, through:)

If you think hard enough, you can remember that moment you invited him in.

(Short pause.)

HUSH: Yes.

LINDA: Yes, what?

PATO: He hides anywhere he can, behind a mask of holiness—especially. Anybody tells you to hate anybody, judge anybody: uhn-un. Anytime you have a mean thought, that's—

(Linda is almost within Hush's reach; he struggles ever harder to avert her gaze, not to see her, to fixate on Pato.)

HUSH: Satan.

LINDA: Satan! Mmm.

PATO: God is love and nothing but love. Nothing else to remember.

HUSH AND PATO: Love.

PATO: Why do you think people go to all those scary movies? That's Satan.

(Linda steps easily within Hush's grasp, her back to him. She drops the towel.

Diane begins whimpering inside the trunk through:)

Inviting us to enjoy the suffering, take part in the slaughter . . . in some small way, get our rocks off on the bullet in the head. We partake of the Devil's food. *(Pause)* Every time I have that urge—to strike, kill, fuck . . . it never goes away . . . ever . . . I promise you . . . I choose. I turn away, say to God, "Help me, I am weak. Take my soul. Use me." . . . That's the only thing I can do in this life, then, is give that to others. It's my . . . answer to all desires.

(Pause.)

HUSH: Thank you.

LINDA: You're welcome.

(Hush is holding his head, fighting against the pull of Linda's nakedness.)

PATO: . . . God's love, man.

HUSH: I mean it.

PATO: I know.

LINDA: I know you do.

(Silence. Hold.)

I know.

(Without warning Hush snaps—he leaps at Linda, who manages to extricate herself, move just outside his reach; the chain catches Hush up short, and he claws at the air between them.

Pato returns to the shadow. Diane's screaming stops abruptly. Linda backs away. Over this, same time:)

Oh, so, *yes!* So . . . *(Short pause)* . . . begins . . . *(Short pause)* . . . man's fall from grace. The voice of Satan: Hate. Vengeance. Let me have it. All. Now. *(Silence)* Don't stop. Let me see your . . . expulsion from the garden. Take, eat, from the apple of . . . knowledge! . . . Mine. You loved me. You loved me, say it—

HUSH: Devil.

LINDA: Yes!

HUSH: You said I gave off power. Electricity. You said I crackled. You knew what you were getting into with me.

LINDA: Oh.

(She is scrambling back into her clothes, a robe, anything.)

HUSH: You sought it out. You knew to be scared. The middle of the night, going nowhere—

LINDA: This is the part I wanted to hear.

HUSH *(Continuous, over)*: —with a stranger.

LINDA: Blame the victim.

HUSH: You knew.

LINDA: After all God didn't mind blaming Eve, did he? Adam too: *she* did it!, she told me to! And the Lord said, "Unto the woman . . . I will greatly multiply thy sorrow! And thy conception! In sorrow thou shalt bring forth children! And thy desire shall be to thy husband, and he shall rule over thee." How . . . fabulous . . . You guys got great ideas from this book, didn't you? It just . . . hits the spot. Even if someone *wants* . . . on some . . . fucking . . . subterranean . . . whatever level . . . to find . . . all they've ever known . . . suffering. That . . . *absolves* you?

HUSH: Forgive yourself.

LINDA: When something . . . terrible happens to you . . . Well, the first time, people are sort of . . . they can be understanding. Not that everyone is. But if terrible things . . . *keep* happening to you . . . if you're sexually abused and then . . . somebody locks you up in a trunk . . . oh, you know, and you can't get better . . . and you . . . lose weight and . . . oh, work and work and work, and save up, and try to get help, and run . . . away and . . . try inflicting it on someone else, and change your whole . . . being . . . fix it all, outside, in . . . cut out part of your *legs* . . . and read every book in the world on *our ancient* clan, the torturers and the tortured . . . Do that and . . . everyone, they all expect you . . . to forget it. I mean . . . if you . . . keep . . . having bad things happen . . . like in a nightmare, a living one . . . the weird thing is that . . . people start to turn away: you're bad luck, you're . . . bringing it on yourself, working out your shit, on some level, they reason . . . you deserve it. Which makes you more alone . . . A friend of mine from childhood . . . the only person I still . . . knew . . . said to me . . . asked me what I might have done in a past life to have to work this out like this . . . in *this* life. Millions and millions of Jews and Gypsies and Roman Catholics all *seeking* the death chambers, tell me what their *karma* required of them, you fucking moron! *(She picks up the knife)* YOU ASSHOLE FUCK SICKO DEVIL, YOU ARE THE DEVIL, I'VE SEEN THE DEVIL IN YOU!

(She rushes him to stab him, and perhaps she cuts him, not grievously, but then they are struggling, and then he has the knife.)

Do it! Do it! Do it! Do it!

(He plunges the knife down; she screams. But he has not stabbed her. Hush clutches his head and prays, fervently, incantatory, the words tumbled together, under:)

HUSH: Get thee behind me. Get thee behind me.

LINDA: Miraculous things! Miraculous things! Are meaningless to me . . . A hummingbird . . . with a red throat . . . quivering . . . flowers . . . it's all . . . nothing. It's all . . . rain . . . it's all . . . love, lovers . . . nothing . . .

HUSH: I'm sorry.

LINDA: I'm sorrier! No one will see! I will be invisible for the rest of my life. You will get all the pity. And you would like me to kill you, that would give you to your God, He will accept you . . . But will He do anything for me?

HUSH: Let me go.

LINDA: I have no God to go to.

HUSH: You are a stranger unto yourself. *(Pause)* Surrender. There is no me, I can't be with you. I can't help you.

LINDA: What????

HUSH: I gave up me—

LINDA: Be *with* me?

HUSH: —don't you understand?, I don't have the courage. I put it all away, all the doubts and memories and wants—

LINDA: With me?

HUSH: I have no me—

LINDA: *So?*

HUSH: You're strong, you can doubt. I can't, I can't want anything, I'll kill it—I'll feel so much, it's all . . . chaos—a welter—what God made the world out of, it wasn't nothing, it was a welter, that's what I am, darkness, and God's made something of me—

LINDA: God's made nothing of you.

HUSH: I don't care, I don't care if it's nothing, I don't care if there is no God, it's the believing that matters, nothing else.

LINDA: Love of another person can be God.

HUSH: I can't save you.

LINDA: Love of one beautiful, most perfect . . .

HUSH: Don't.

LINDA: . . . mouth, eyes . . .

HUSH: Not a *moment* I haven't thought of you. You. It's too much . . . It's a hell of wanting. Save me. Please. Jesus.

(She cradles his head, stroking his hair; but he is lost to his voices.)

LINDA: Years. Planning. For this. To tempt you with cash. My cabin in the woods. If you figured it out right away, I would pull the lever, because I'd arranged to get us an exit row. There would be no escape for you. *(Short pause)* But I'm the one . . .

HUSH: Choose.

LINDA: I'm sorry I took away your drugs . . . God forgive me . . .

HUSH: Accept Him. *(Pause)* In your heart.

LINDA: I have no heart, Hush.

HUSH: Choose. No matter *what* . . . mankind always possesses the choice. It's never over.

LINDA: I think you should go . . . I think . . . that I still . . . very much want to see you destroyed and I want to be destroyed . . . And . . . I still . . . love you, Hush.

HUSH: I know.

LINDA: I love you so . . . There will never . . .

HUSH: I know.

LINDA: Be . . . another man for me . . .

HUSH: I know.

LINDA: So . . . you go . . .

(Pause. She unlocks Hush's manacles. He moves to gather his belongings.)

HUSH: You can choose. You can. You can.
LINDA: Kill me. Please. I'm begging you.

(He starts to exit; she holds him back.)

Please, end this. End it! End it!

(He grabs her.)

You love me.

(It seems he might kiss her, his hands around her neck, but he lifts her, and shoves her slowly down onto the bed, strangling her with:)

HUSH: Yes. *(Again)* Yes. *(Again)* Yes.
LINDA: Please.
HUSH: Yes.

(Hold. Hush struggles against the voices, she is moving toward peace. Hush releases her.)

LINDA: No! . . . You can't.
HUSH: I forgive you.
LINDA: You can't—
HUSH: I forgive—
LINDA: —do this to me. You can't choose that, you can't triumph over that.
HUSH: Christ forgives us. He forgives us our trespasses as we have trespassed against them.
LINDA: You cannot . . .
HUSH: Even if He isn't there He does it.
LINDA: . . . oh, no . . . no . . .
HUSH: I'll call an ambulance.

LINDA: I'll be gone.
HUSH: Save yourself.
LINDA: I'll kill myself.
HUSH: I can't—
LINDA: I will Hush: I'll call . . .

(He is gone.)

LINDA: GET IN THE TRUNK! GET IN THE TRUNK!
GET IN THE TRUNK! YOU OOOOOWWWWW-
WWWWWWE ME! *(Silence)* Choose. I have choices.
I have choices. Yes. I accept Christ in my heart. *(Pause)*
. . . Choices . . . *(She starts to clean up, leaving the knife
for last; she picks it up)* I can choose. *(She grips it tight,
walking, struggling)* I can choose . . . I have choices . . .
(She stabs it into the cutting board, walks away) . . . Hush
. . . I have choices. *(She sits, breathes)* So many choices.
Okay. *(She gets up, goes to the trunk, opens it. Pause)*
I have choices. *(She gets in. Silence)* I can choose.
*(Silence. She at last reaches up and takes hold of the top of
the trunk and shuts it with a slam. From within the trunk
she starts to scream. And scream)* Help! HELP! HELP!
HELP ME! SOMEBODY HELP ME! HELP ME!

END OF PLAY